Mastering Linux - Security

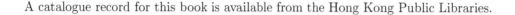

A catalogue record for this book is available from the Hong Kong Public Libraries.

Published in Hong Kong by Samurai Media Limited.

Email: info@samuraimedia.org

ISBN 978-988-8406-20-3

Background Cover Image by https://www.flickr.com/people/webtreatsetc/

Table of Contents

List of Tables

Part I. local user management

Table of Contents

Chapter 1. introduction to users

This little chapter will teach you how to identify your user account on a Unix computer using commands like **who am i**, **id**, and more.

In a second part you will learn how to become another user with the **su** command.

And you will learn how to run a program as another user with **sudo**.

1.1. whoami

The **whoami** command tells you your username.

```
[paul@centos7 ~]$ whoami
paul
[paul@centos7 ~]$
```

1.2. who

The **who** command will give you information about who is logged on the system.

```
[paul@centos7 ~]$ who
root     pts/0        2014-10-10 23:07 (10.104.33.101)
paul     pts/1        2014-10-10 23:30 (10.104.33.101)
laura    pts/2        2014-10-10 23:34 (10.104.33.96)
tania    pts/3        2014-10-10 23:39 (10.104.33.91)
[paul@centos7 ~]$
```

1.3. who am i

With **who am i** the **who** command will display only the line pointing to your current session.

```
[paul@centos7 ~]$ who am i
paul     pts/1        2014-10-10 23:30 (10.104.33.101)
[paul@centos7 ~]$
```

1.4. w

The **w** command shows you who is logged on and what they are doing.

```
[paul@centos7 ~]$ w
 23:34:07 up 31 min,  2 users,  load average: 0.00, 0.01, 0.02
USER     TTY        LOGIN@   IDLE   JCPU   PCPU WHAT
root     pts/0      23:07    15.00s 0.01s  0.01s top
paul     pts/1      23:30    7.00s  0.00s  0.00s w
[paul@centos7 ~]$
```

1.5. id

The **id** command will give you your user id, primary group id, and a list of the groups that you belong to.

```
paul@debian7:~$ id
uid=1000(paul) gid=1000(paul) groups=1000(paul)
```

On RHEL/CentOS you will also get **SELinux** context information with this command.

```
[root@centos7 ~]# id
uid=0(root) gid=0(root) groups=0(root) context=unconfined_u:unconfined_r\
:unconfined_t:s0-s0:c0.c1023
```

1.6. su to another user

The **su** command allows a user to run a shell as another user.

```
laura@debian7:~$ su tania
Password:
tania@debian7:/home/laura$
```

1.7. su to root

Yes you can also **su** to become **root**, when you know the **root password**.

```
laura@debian7:~$ su root
Password:
root@debian7:/home/laura#
```

1.8. su as root

You need to know the password of the user you want to substitute to, unless your are logged in as **root**. The **root** user can become any existing user without knowing that user's password.

```
root@debian7:~# id
uid=0(root) gid=0(root) groups=0(root)
root@debian7:~# su - valentina
valentina@debian7:~$
```

1.9. su - $username

By default, the **su** command maintains the same shell environment. To become another user and also get the target user's environment, issue the **su -** command followed by the target username.

```
root@debian7:~# su laura
laura@debian7:/root$ exit
exit
root@debian7:~# su - laura
laura@debian7:~$ pwd
/home/laura
```

1.10. su -

When no username is provided to **su** or **su -**, the command will assume **root** is the target.

```
tania@debian7:~$ su -
Password:
root@debian7:~#
```

1.11. run a program as another user

The sudo program allows a user to start a program with the credentials of another user. Before this works, the system administrator has to set up the **/etc/sudoers** file. This can be useful to delegate administrative tasks to another user (without giving the root password).

The screenshot below shows the usage of **sudo**. User **paul** received the right to run **useradd** with the credentials of **root**. This allows **paul** to create new users on the system without becoming **root** and without knowing the **root password**.

First the command fails for **paul**.

```
paul@debian7:~$ /usr/sbin/useradd -m valentina
useradd: Permission denied.
useradd: cannot lock /etc/passwd; try again later.
```

But with **sudo** it works.

```
paul@debian7:~$ sudo /usr/sbin/useradd -m valentina
[sudo] password for paul:
paul@debian7:~$
```

1.12. visudo

Check the man page of **visudo** before playing with the **/etc/sudoers** file. Editing the **sudoers** is out of scope for this fundamentals book.

```
paul@rhel65:~$ apropos visudo
visudo              (8)  - edit the sudoers file
paul@rhel65:~$
```

1.13. sudo su -

On some Linux systems like Ubuntu and Xubuntu, the **root** user does not have a password set. This means that it is not possible to login as **root** (extra security). To perform tasks as **root**, the first user is given all **sudo rights** via the **/etc/sudoers**. In fact all users that are members of the admin group can use sudo to run all commands as root.

```
root@laika:~# grep admin /etc/sudoers
# Members of the admin group may gain root privileges
%admin ALL=(ALL) ALL
```

The end result of this is that the user can type **sudo su -** and become root without having to enter the root password. The sudo command does require you to enter your own password. Thus the password prompt in the screenshot below is for sudo, not for su.

```
paul@laika:~$ sudo su -
Password:
root@laika:~#
```

1.14. sudo logging

Using **sudo** without authorization will result in a severe warning:

```
paul@rhel65:~$ sudo su -

We trust you have received the usual lecture from the local System
Administrator. It usually boils down to these three things:

    #1) Respect the privacy of others.
    #2) Think before you type.
    #3) With great power comes great responsibility.

[sudo] password for paul:
paul is not in the sudoers file.  This incident will be reported.
paul@rhel65:~$
```

The root user can see this in the **/var/log/secure** on Red Hat and in **/var/log/auth.log** on Debian).

```
root@rhel65:~# tail /var/log/secure | grep sudo | tr -s ' '
Apr 13 16:03:42 rhel65 sudo: paul : user NOT in sudoers ; TTY=pts/0 ; PWD=\
/home/paul ; USER=root ; COMMAND=/bin/su -
root@rhel65:~#
```

1.15. practice: introduction to users

1. Run a command that displays only your currently logged on user name.

2. Display a list of all logged on users.

3. Display a list of all logged on users including the command they are running at this very moment.

4. Display your user name and your unique user identification (userid).

5. Use **su** to switch to another user account (unless you are root, you will need the password of the other account). And get back to the previous account.

6. Now use **su -** to switch to another user and notice the difference.

Note that **su -** gets you into the home directory of **Tania**.

7. Try to create a new user account (when using your normal user account). this should fail. (Details on adding user accounts are explained in the next chapter.)

8. Now try the same, but with **sudo** before your command.

1.16. solution: introduction to users

1. Run a command that displays only your currently logged on user name.

```
laura@debian7:~$ whoami
laura
laura@debian7:~$ echo $USER
laura
```

2. Display a list of all logged on users.

```
laura@debian7:~$ who
laura      pts/0        2014-10-13 07:22 (10.104.33.101)
laura@debian7:~$
```

3. Display a list of all logged on users including the command they are running at this very moment.

```
laura@debian7:~$ w
 07:47:02 up 16 min,  2 users,  load average: 0.00, 0.00, 0.00
USER     TTY      FROM            LOGIN@   IDLE   JCPU   PCPU WHAT
root     pts/0    10.104.33.101   07:30    6.00s  0.04s  0.00s w
root     pts/1    10.104.33.101   07:46    6.00s  0.01s  0.00s sleep 42
laura@debian7:~$
```

4. Display your user name and your unique user identification (userid).

```
laura@debian7:~$ id
uid=1005(laura) gid=1007(laura) groups=1007(laura)
laura@debian7:~$
```

5. Use **su** to switch to another user account (unless you are root, you will need the password of the other account). And get back to the previous account.

```
laura@debian7:~$ su tania
Password:
tania@debian7:/home/laura$ id
uid=1006(tania) gid=1008(tania) groups=1008(tania)
tania@debian7:/home/laura$ exit
laura@debian7:~$
```

6. Now use **su -** to switch to another user and notice the difference.

```
laura@debian7:~$ su - tania
Password:
tania@debian7:~$ pwd
/home/tania
tania@debian7:~$ logout
laura@debian7:~$
```

Note that **su -** gets you into the home directory of **Tania**.

7. Try to create a new user account (when using your normal user account). this should fail. (Details on adding user accounts are explained in the next chapter.)

```
laura@debian7:~$ useradd valentina
-su: useradd: command not found
laura@debian7:~$ /usr/sbin/useradd valentina
useradd: Permission denied.
useradd: cannot lock /etc/passwd; try again later.
```

It is possible that **useradd** is located in **/sbin/useradd** on your computer.

8. Now try the same, but with **sudo** before your command.

```
laura@debian7:~$ sudo /usr/sbin/useradd valentina
[sudo] password for laura:
laura is not in the sudoers file.  This incident will be reported.
laura@debian7:~$
```

Notice that **laura** has no permission to use the **sudo** on this system.

Chapter 2. user management

This chapter will teach you how to use **useradd**, **usermod** and **userdel** to create, modify and remove user accounts.

You will need **root** access on a Linux computer to complete this chapter.

2.1. user management

User management on Linux can be done in three complementary ways. You can use the **graphical** tools provided by your distribution. These tools have a look and feel that depends on the distribution. If you are a novice Linux user on your home system, then use the graphical tool that is provided by your distribution. This will make sure that you do not run into problems.

Another option is to use **command line tools** like useradd, usermod, gpasswd, passwd and others. Server administrators are likely to use these tools, since they are familiar and very similar across many different distributions. This chapter will focus on these command line tools.

A third and rather extremist way is to **edit the local configuration files** directly using vi (or vipw/vigr). Do not attempt this as a novice on production systems!

2.2. /etc/passwd

The local user database on Linux (and on most Unixes) is **/etc/passwd**.

```
[root@RHEL5 ~]# tail /etc/passwd
inge:x:518:524:art dealer:/home/inge:/bin/ksh
ann:x:519:525:flute player:/home/ann:/bin/bash
frederik:x:520:526:rubius poet:/home/frederik:/bin/bash
steven:x:521:527:roman emperor:/home/steven:/bin/bash
pascale:x:522:528:artist:/home/pascale:/bin/ksh
geert:x:524:530:kernel developer:/home/geert:/bin/bash
wim:x:525:531:master damuti:/home/wim:/bin/bash
sandra:x:526:532:radish stresser:/home/sandra:/bin/bash
annelies:x:527:533:sword fighter:/home/annelies:/bin/bash
laura:x:528:534:art dealer:/home/laura:/bin/ksh
```

As you can see, this file contains seven columns separated by a colon. The columns contain the username, an x, the user id, the primary group id, a description, the name of the home directory, and the login shell.

More information can be found by typing **man 5 passwd**.

```
[root@RHEL5 ~]# man 5 passwd
```

2.3. root

The **root** user also called the **superuser** is the most powerful account on your Linux system. This user can do almost anything, including the creation of other users. The root user always has userid 0 (regardless of the name of the account).

```
[root@RHEL5 ~]# head -1 /etc/passwd
root:x:0:0:root:/root:/bin/bash
```

2.4. useradd

You can add users with the **useradd** command. The example below shows how to add a user named yanina (last parameter) and at the same time forcing the creation of the home directory (-m), setting the name of the home directory (-d), and setting a description (-c).

```
[root@RHEL5 ~]# useradd -m -d /home/yanina -c "yanina wickmayer" yanina
[root@RHEL5 ~]# tail -1 /etc/passwd
yanina:x:529:529:yanina wickmayer:/home/yanina:/bin/bash
```

The user named yanina received userid 529 and **primary group** id 529.

2.5. /etc/default/useradd

Both Red Hat Enterprise Linux and Debian/Ubuntu have a file called **/etc/default/useradd** that contains some default user options. Besides using cat to display this file, you can also use **useradd -D**.

```
[root@RHEL4 ~]# useradd -D
GROUP=100
HOME=/home
INACTIVE=-1
EXPIRE=
SHELL=/bin/bash
SKEL=/etc/skel
```

2.6. userdel

You can delete the user yanina with **userdel**. The -r option of userdel will also remove the home directory.

```
[root@RHEL5 ~]# userdel -r yanina
```

2.7. usermod

You can modify the properties of a user with the **usermod** command. This example uses **usermod** to change the description of the user harry.

```
[root@RHEL4 ~]# tail -1 /etc/passwd
harry:x:516:520:harry potter:/home/harry:/bin/bash
[root@RHEL4 ~]# usermod -c 'wizard' harry
[root@RHEL4 ~]# tail -1 /etc/passwd
harry:x:516:520:wizard:/home/harry:/bin/bash
```

2.8. creating home directories

The easiest way to create a home directory is to supply the **-m** option with **useradd** (it is likely set as a default option on Linux).

A less easy way is to create a home directory manually with **mkdir** which also requires setting the owner and the permissions on the directory with **chmod** and **chown** (both commands are discussed in detail in another chapter).

```
[root@RHEL5 ~]# mkdir /home/laura
[root@RHEL5 ~]# chown laura:laura /home/laura
[root@RHEL5 ~]# chmod 700 /home/laura
[root@RHEL5 ~]# ls -ld /home/laura/
drwx------ 2 laura laura 4096 Jun 24 15:17 /home/laura/
```

2.9. /etc/skel/

When using **useradd** the **-m** option, the **/etc/skel/** directory is copied to the newly created home directory. The **/etc/skel/** directory contains some (usually hidden) files that contain profile settings and default values for applications. In this way **/etc/skel/** serves as a default home directory and as a default user profile.

```
[root@RHEL5 ~]# ls -la /etc/skel/
total 48
drwxr-xr-x  2 root root  4096 Apr  1 00:11 .
drwxr-xr-x 97 root root 12288 Jun 24 15:36 ..
-rw-r--r--  1 root root    24 Jul 12  2006 .bash_logout
-rw-r--r--  1 root root   176 Jul 12  2006 .bash_profile
-rw-r--r--  1 root root   124 Jul 12  2006 .bashrc
```

2.10. deleting home directories

The -r option of **userdel** will make sure that the home directory is deleted together with the user account.

```
[root@RHEL5 ~]# ls -ld /home/wim/
drwx------ 2 wim wim 4096 Jun 24 15:19 /home/wim/
[root@RHEL5 ~]# userdel -r wim
[root@RHEL5 ~]# ls -ld /home/wim/
ls: /home/wim/: No such file or directory
```

2.11. login shell

The **/etc/passwd** file specifies the **login shell** for the user. In the screenshot below you can see that user annelies will log in with the **/bin/bash** shell, and user laura with the **/bin/ksh** shell.

```
[root@RHEL5 ~]# tail -2 /etc/passwd
annelies:x:527:533:sword fighter:/home/annelies:/bin/bash
laura:x:528:534:art dealer:/home/laura:/bin/ksh
```

You can use the usermod command to change the shell for a user.

```
[root@RHEL5 ~]# usermod -s /bin/bash laura
[root@RHEL5 ~]# tail -1 /etc/passwd
laura:x:528:534:art dealer:/home/laura:/bin/bash
```

2.12. chsh

Users can change their login shell with the **chsh** command. First, user harry obtains a list of available shells (he could also have done a **cat /etc/shells**) and then changes his login shell to the **Korn shell** (/bin/ksh). At the next login, harry will default into ksh instead of bash.

```
[laura@centos7 ~]$ chsh -l
/bin/sh
/bin/bash
/sbin/nologin
/usr/bin/sh
/usr/bin/bash
/usr/sbin/nologin
/bin/ksh
/bin/tcsh
/bin/csh
[laura@centos7 ~]$
```

Note that the **-l** option does not exist on Debian and that the above screenshot assumes that **ksh** and **csh** shells are installed.

The screenshot below shows how **laura** can change her default shell (active on next login).

```
[laura@centos7 ~]$ chsh -s /bin/ksh
Changing shell for laura.
Password:
Shell changed.
```

2.13. practice: user management

1. Create a user account named **serena**, including a home directory and a description (or comment) that reads **Serena Williams**. Do all this in one single command.

2. Create a user named **venus**, including home directory, bash shell, a description that reads **Venus Williams** all in one single command.

3. Verify that both users have correct entries in **/etc/passwd**, **/etc/shadow** and **/etc/group**.

4. Verify that their home directory was created.

5. Create a user named **einstime** with **/bin/date** as his default logon shell.

7. What happens when you log on with the **einstime** user ? Can you think of a useful real world example for changing a user's login shell to an application ?

8. Create a file named **welcome.txt** and make sure every new user will see this file in their home directory.

9. Verify this setup by creating (and deleting) a test user account.

10. Change the default login shell for the **serena** user to **/bin/bash**. Verify before and after you make this change.

2.14. solution: user management

1. Create a user account named **serena**, including a home directory and a description (or comment) that reads **Serena Williams**. Do all this in one single command.

```
root@debian7:~# useradd -m -c 'Serena Williams' serena
```

2. Create a user named **venus**, including home directory, bash shell, a description that reads **Venus Williams** all in one single command.

```
root@debian7:~# useradd -m -c "Venus Williams" -s /bin/bash venus
```

3. Verify that both users have correct entries in **/etc/passwd**, **/etc/shadow** and **/etc/group**.

```
root@debian7:~# tail -2 /etc/passwd
serena:x:1008:1010:Serena Williams:/home/serena:/bin/sh
venus:x:1009:1011:Venus Williams:/home/venus:/bin/bash
root@debian7:~# tail -2 /etc/shadow
serena:!:16358:0:99999:7:::
venus:!:16358:0:99999:7:::
root@debian7:~# tail -2 /etc/group
serena:x:1010:
venus:x:1011:
```

4. Verify that their home directory was created.

```
root@debian7:~# ls -lrt /home | tail -2
drwxr-xr-x 2 serena      serena      4096 Oct 15 10:50 serena
drwxr-xr-x 2 venus       venus       4096 Oct 15 10:59 venus
root@debian7:~#
```

5. Create a user named **einstime** with **/bin/date** as his default logon shell.

```
root@debian7:~# useradd -s /bin/date einstime
```

Or even better:

```
root@debian7:~# useradd -s $(which date) einstime
```

7. What happens when you log on with the **einstime** user ? Can you think of a useful real world example for changing a user's login shell to an application ?

```
root@debian7:~# su - einstime
Wed Oct 15 11:05:56 UTC 2014 # You get the output of the date command
root@debian7:~#
```

It can be useful when users need to access only one application on the server. Just logging in opens the application for them, and closing the application automatically logs them out.

8. Create a file named **welcome.txt** and make sure every new user will see this file in their home directory.

```
root@debian7:~# echo Hello > /etc/skel/welcome.txt
```

9. Verify this setup by creating (and deleting) a test user account.

```
root@debian7:~# useradd -m test
root@debian7:~# ls -l /home/test
total 4
-rw-r--r-- 1 test test 6 Oct 15 11:16 welcome.txt
root@debian7:~# userdel -r test
root@debian7:~#
```

10. Change the default login shell for the **serena** user to **/bin/bash**. Verify before and after you make this change.

```
root@debian7:~# grep serena /etc/passwd
serena:x:1008:1010:Serena Williams:/home/serena:/bin/sh
root@debian7:~# usermod -s /bin/bash serena
root@debian7:~# grep serena /etc/passwd
serena:x:1008:1010:Serena Williams:/home/serena:/bin/bash
root@debian7:~#
```

Chapter 3. user passwords

This chapter will tell you more about passwords for local users.

Three methods for setting passwords are explained; using the **passwd** command, using **openssel passwd**, and using the **crypt** function in a C program.

The chapter will also discuss password settings and disabling, suspending or locking accounts.

3.1. passwd

Passwords of users can be set with the **passwd** command. Users will have to provide their old password before twice entering the new one.

```
[tania@centos7 ~]$ passwd
Changing password for user tania.
Changing password for tania.
(current) UNIX password:
New password:
BAD PASSWORD: The password is shorter than 8 characters
New password:
BAD PASSWORD: The password is a palindrome
New password:
BAD PASSWORD: The password is too similar to the old one
passwd: Have exhausted maximum number of retries for service
```

As you can see, the passwd tool will do some basic verification to prevent users from using too simple passwords. The **root** user does not have to follow these rules (there will be a warning though). The **root** user also does not have to provide the old password before entering the new password twice.

```
root@debian7:~# passwd tania
Enter new UNIX password:
Retype new UNIX password:
passwd: password updated successfully
```

3.2. shadow file

User passwords are encrypted and kept in **/etc/shadow**. The /etc/shadow file is read only and can only be read by root. We will see in the file permissions section how it is possible for users to change their password. For now, you will have to know that users can change their password with the **/usr/bin/passwd** command.

```
[root@centos7 ~]# tail -4 /etc/shadow
paul:$6$ikp2Xta5BT.Tml.p$2TZjNnOYNNQKpwLJqoGJbVsZG5/Fti8ovBRd.VzRbiDS17TEq\
IaSMH.TeBKnTS/SjlMruW8qffC0JNORW.BTW1:16338:0:99999:7:::
tania:$6$8Z/zovxj$9qvoqT8i9KIrmN.k4EQwAF5ryz5yzNwEvYjAa9L5XVXQu.z4DlpvMREH\
eQpQzvRnqFdKkVj17H5ST.c79HDZw0:16356:0:99999:7:::
laura:$6$glDuTY5e$/NYYWLxfHgZFWeoujaXSMcR.Mz.1GOxtcxFocFVJNb98nbTPhWFXfKWG\
SyYh1WCv6763Wq54.w24Yr3uAZBOm/:16356:0:99999:7:::
valentina:$6$jrZa6PVI$1uQgqR6En9mZB6mKJ3LXRB4CnFko6LRhbh.v4iqUk9MVreui1lv7\
GxHOUDSKA0N55ZRNhGHa6T2ouFnVno/0o1:16356:0:99999:7:::
[root@centos7 ~]#
```

The **/etc/shadow** file contains nine colon separated columns. The nine fields contain (from left to right) the user name, the encrypted password (note that only inge and laura have an encrypted password), the day the password was last changed (day 1 is January 1, 1970), number of days the password must be left unchanged, password expiry day, warning number of days before password expiry, number of days after expiry before disabling the account, and the day the account was disabled (again, since 1970). The last field has no meaning yet.

All the passwords in the screenshot above are hashes of **hunter2**.

3.3. encryption with passwd

Passwords are stored in an encrypted format. This encryption is done by the **crypt** function. The easiest (and recommended) way to add a user with a password to the system is to add the user with the **useradd -m user** command, and then set the user's password with **passwd**.

```
[root@RHEL4 ~]# useradd -m xavier
[root@RHEL4 ~]# passwd xavier
Changing password for user xavier.
New UNIX password:
Retype new UNIX password:
passwd: all authentication tokens updated successfully.
[root@RHEL4 ~]#
```

3.4. encryption with openssl

Another way to create users with a password is to use the -p option of useradd, but that option requires an encrypted password. You can generate this encrypted password with the **openssl passwd** command.

The **openssl passwd** command will generate several distinct hashes for the same password, for this it uses a **salt**.

```
paul@rhel65:~$ openssl passwd hunter2
86jcUNlnGDFpY
paul@rhel65:~$ openssl passwd hunter2
Yj7mDO9OAnvq6
paul@rhel65:~$ openssl passwd hunter2
YqDcJeGoDbzKA
paul@rhel65:~$
```

This **salt** can be chosen and is visible as the first two characters of the hash.

```
paul@rhel65:~$ openssl passwd -salt 42 hunter2
42ZrbtP1Ze8G.
paul@rhel65:~$ openssl passwd -salt 42 hunter2
42ZrbtP1Ze8G.
paul@rhel65:~$ openssl passwd -salt 42 hunter2
42ZrbtP1Ze8G.
paul@rhel65:~$
```

This example shows how to create a user with password.

```
root@rhel65:~# useradd -m -p $(openssl passwd hunter2) mohamed
```

Note that this command puts the password in your command history!

3.5. encryption with crypt

A third option is to create your own C program using the crypt function, and compile this into a command.

```
paul@rhel65:~$ cat MyCrypt.c
#include <stdio.h>
#define __USE_XOPEN
#include <unistd.h>

int main(int argc, char** argv)
{
 if(argc==3)
    {
        printf("%s\n", crypt(argv[1],argv[2]));
    }
    else
    {
        printf("Usage: MyCrypt $password $salt\n" );
    }
   return 0;
}
```

This little program can be compiled with **gcc** like this.

```
paul@rhel65:~$ gcc MyCrypt.c -o MyCrypt -lcrypt
```

To use it, we need to give two parameters to MyCrypt. The first is the unencrypted password, the second is the salt. The salt is used to perturb the encryption algorithm in one of 4096 different ways. This variation prevents two users with the same password from having the same entry in **/etc/shadow**.

```
paul@rhel65:~$ ./MyCrypt hunter2 42
42ZrbtP1Ze8G.
paul@rhel65:~$ ./MyCrypt hunter2 33
33d6taYSiEUXI
```

Did you notice that the first two characters of the password are the **salt**?

The standard output of the crypt function is using the DES algorithm which is old and can be cracked in minutes. A better method is to use **md5** passwords which can be recognized by a salt starting with 1.

```
paul@rhel65:~$ ./MyCrypt hunter2 '$1$42'
$1$42$716Y3xT5282XmZrtDOF9f0
paul@rhel65:~$ ./MyCrypt hunter2 '$6$42'
$6$42$OqFFAVnI3gTSYG0yI9TZWX9cpyQzwIop7HwpG1LLEsNBiMr4w6OvLX1KDa./UpwXfrFk1i...
```

The **md5** salt can be up to eight characters long. The salt is displayed in **/etc/shadow** between the second and third $, so never use the password as the salt!

```
paul@rhel65:~$ ./MyCrypt hunter2 '$1$hunter2'
$1$hunter2$YVxrxDmidq7Xf8Gdt6qM2.
```

3.6. /etc/login.defs

The **/etc/login.defs** file contains some default settings for user passwords like password aging and length settings. (You will also find the numerical limits of user ids and group ids and whether or not a home directory should be created by default).

```
root@rhel65:~# grep ^PASS /etc/login.defs
PASS_MAX_DAYS    99999
PASS_MIN_DAYS    0
PASS_MIN_LEN     5
PASS_WARN_AGE    7
```

Debian also has this file.

```
root@debian7:~# grep PASS /etc/login.defs
#   PASS_MAX_DAYS    Maximum number of days a password may be used.
#   PASS_MIN_DAYS    Minimum number of days allowed between password changes.
#   PASS_WARN_AGE    Number of days warning given before a password expires.
PASS_MAX_DAYS    99999
PASS_MIN_DAYS    0
PASS_WARN_AGE    7
#PASS_CHANGE_TRIES
#PASS_ALWAYS_WARN
#PASS_MIN_LEN
#PASS_MAX_LEN
# NO_PASSWORD_CONSOLE
root@debian7:~#
```

3.7. chage

The **chage** command can be used to set an expiration date for a user account (-E), set a minimum (-m) and maximum (-M) password age, a password expiration date, and set the number of warning days before the password expiration date. Much of this functionality is also available from the **passwd** command. The **-l** option of chage will list these settings for a user.

```
root@rhel65:~# chage -l paul
Last password change                                    : Mar 27, 2014
Password expires                                        : never
Password inactive                                       : never
Account expires                                         : never
Minimum number of days between password change          : 0
Maximum number of days between password change          : 99999
Number of days of warning before password expires       : 7
root@rhel65:~#
```

3.8. disabling a password

Passwords in **/etc/shadow** cannot begin with an exclamation mark. When the second field in **/etc/passwd** starts with an exclamation mark, then the password can not be used.

Using this feature is often called **locking**, **disabling**, or **suspending** a user account. Besides **vi** (or vipw) you can also accomplish this with **usermod**.

The first command in the next screenshot will show the hashed password of **laura** in **/etc/shadow**. The next command disables the password of **laura**, making it impossible for Laura to authenticate using this password.

```
root@debian7:~# grep laura /etc/shadow | cut -c1-70
laura:$6$JYj4JZqp$stwwWACp3OtE1R2aZuE87j.nbW.puDkNUYVk7mCHfCVMa3CoDUJV
root@debian7:~# usermod -L laura
```

As you can see below, the password hash is simply preceded with an exclamation mark.

```
root@debian7:~# grep laura /etc/shadow | cut -c1-70
laura:!$6$JYj4JZqp$stwwWACp3OtE1R2aZuE87j.nbW.puDkNUYVk7mCHfCVMa3CoDUJ
root@debian7:~#
```

The root user (and users with **sudo** rights on **su**) still will be able to **su** into the **laura** account (because the password is not needed here). Also note that **laura** will still be able to login if she has set up passwordless ssh!

```
root@debian7:~# su - laura
laura@debian7:~$
```

You can unlock the account again with **usermod -U**.

```
root@debian7:~# usermod -U laura
root@debian7:~# grep laura /etc/shadow | cut -c1-70
laura:$6$JYj4JZqp$stwwWACp3OtE1R2aZuE87j.nbW.puDkNUYVk7mCHfCVMa3CoDUJV
```

Watch out for tiny differences in the command line options of **passwd**, **usermod**, and **useradd** on different Linux distributions. Verify the local files when using features like **"disabling, suspending, or locking"** on user accounts and their passwords.

3.9. editing local files

If you still want to manually edit the **/etc/passwd** or **/etc/shadow**, after knowing these commands for password management, then use **vipw** instead of vi(m) directly. The **vipw** tool will do proper locking of the file.

```
[root@RHEL5 ~]# vipw /etc/passwd
vipw: the password file is busy (/etc/ptmp present)
```

3.10. practice: user passwords

1. Set the password for **serena** to **hunter2**.

2. Also set a password for **venus** and then lock the **venus** user account with **usermod**. Verify the locking in **/etc/shadow** before and after you lock it.

3. Use **passwd -d** to disable the **serena** password. Verify the **serena** line in **/etc/shadow** before and after disabling.

4. What is the difference between locking a user account and disabling a user account's password like we just did with **usermod -L** and **passwd -d**?

5. Try changing the password of serena to serena as serena.

6. Make sure **serena** has to change her password in 10 days.

7. Make sure every new user needs to change their password every 10 days.

8. Take a backup as root of **/etc/shadow**. Use **vi** to copy an encrypted **hunter2** hash from **venus** to **serena**. Can **serena** now log on with **hunter2** as a password ?

9. Why use **vipw** instead of **vi** ? What could be the problem when using **vi** or **vim** ?

10. Use **chsh** to list all shells (only works on RHEL/CentOS/Fedora), and compare to **cat /etc/shells**.

11. Which **useradd** option allows you to name a home directory ?

12. How can you see whether the password of user **serena** is locked or unlocked ? Give a solution with **grep** and a solution with **passwd**.

3.11. solution: user passwords

1. Set the password for **serena** to **hunter2**.

```
root@debian7:~# passwd serena
Enter new UNIX password:
Retype new UNIX password:
passwd: password updated successfully
```

2. Also set a password for **venus** and then lock the **venus** user account with **usermod**. Verify the locking in **/etc/shadow** before and after you lock it.

```
root@debian7:~# passwd venus
Enter new UNIX password:
Retype new UNIX password:
passwd: password updated successfully
root@debian7:~# grep venus /etc/shadow | cut -c1-70
venus:$6$gswzXICW$uSnKFV1kFKZmTPaMVS4AvNA/KO27OxN0v5LHdV9ed0gTyXrjUeM/
root@debian7:~# usermod -L venus
root@debian7:~# grep venus /etc/shadow | cut -c1-70
venus:!$6$gswzXICW$uSnKFV1kFKZmTPaMVS4AvNA/KO27OxN0v5LHdV9ed0gTyXrjUeM
```

Note that **usermod -L** precedes the password hash with an exclamation mark (!).

3. Use **passwd -d** to disable the **serena** password. Verify the **serena** line in **/etc/shadow** before and after disabling.

```
root@debian7:~# grep serena /etc/shadow | cut -c1-70
serena:$6$Es/omrPE$F2Ypu8kpLrfKdW0v/UIwA5jrYyBD2nwZ/dt.i/IypRgiPZSdB/B
root@debian7:~# passwd -d serena
passwd: password expiry information changed.
root@debian7:~# grep serena /etc/shadow
serena::16358:0:99999:7:::
root@debian7:~#
```

4. What is the difference between locking a user account and disabling a user account's password like we just did with **usermod -L** and **passwd -d**?

Locking will prevent the user from logging on to the system with his password by putting a ! in front of the password in **/etc/shadow**.

Disabling with **passwd** will erase the password from **/etc/shadow**.

5. Try changing the password of serena to serena as serena.

```
log on as serena, then execute: passwd serena... it should fail!
```

6. Make sure **serena** has to change her password in 10 days.

```
chage -M 10 serena
```

7. Make sure every new user needs to change their password every 10 days.

```
vi /etc/login.defs (and change PASS_MAX_DAYS to 10)
```

8. Take a backup as root of **/etc/shadow**. Use **vi** to copy an encrypted **hunter2** hash from **venus** to **serena**. Can **serena** now log on with **hunter2** as a password ?

```
Yes.
```

9. Why use **vipw** instead of **vi** ? What could be the problem when using **vi** or **vim** ?

`vipw` will give a warning when someone else is already using that file (with `vipw`).

10. Use **chsh** to list all shells (only works on RHEL/CentOS/Fedora), and compare to **cat / etc/shells**.

```
chsh -l
cat /etc/shells
```

11. Which **useradd** option allows you to name a home directory ?

```
-d
```

12. How can you see whether the password of user **serena** is locked or unlocked ? Give a solution with **grep** and a solution with **passwd**.

```
grep serena /etc/shadow
```

```
passwd -S serena
```

Chapter 4. user profiles

Logged on users have a number of preset (and customized) aliases, variables, and functions, but where do they come from ? The **shell** uses a number of startup files that are executed (or rather **sourced**) whenever the shell is invoked. What follows is an overview of startup scripts.

4.1. system profile

Both the **bash** and the **ksh** shell will verify the existence of **/etc/profile** and **source** it if it exists.

When reading this script, you will notice (both on Debian and on Red Hat Enterprise Linux) that it builds the PATH environment variable (among others). The script might also change the PS1 variable, set the HOSTNAME and execute even more scripts like **/etc/inputrc**

This screenshot uses grep to show PATH manipulation in **/etc/profile** on Debian.

```
root@debian7:~# grep PATH /etc/profile
  PATH="/usr/local/sbin:/usr/local/bin:/usr/sbin:/usr/bin:/sbin:/bin"
  PATH="/usr/local/bin:/usr/bin:/bin:/usr/local/games:/usr/games"
export PATH
root@debian7:~#
```

This screenshot uses grep to show PATH manipulation in **/etc/profile** on RHEL7/CentOS7.

```
[root@centos7 ~]# grep PATH /etc/profile
    case ":${PATH}:" in
                PATH=$PATH:$1
                PATH=$1:$PATH
export PATH USER LOGNAME MAIL HOSTNAME HISTSIZE HISTCONTROL
[root@centos7 ~]#
```

The **root user** can use this script to set aliases, functions, and variables for every user on the system.

4.2. ~/.bash_profile

When this file exists in the home directory, then **bash** will source it. On Debian Linux 5/6/7 this file does not exist by default.

RHEL7/CentOS7 uses a small ~/.**bash_profile** where it checks for the existence of ~/.**bashrc** and then sources it. It also adds $HOME/bin to the $PATH variable.

```
[root@rhel7 ~]# cat /home/paul/.bash_profile
# .bash_profile

# Get the aliases and functions
if [ -f ~/.bashrc ]; then
        . ~/.bashrc
fi

# User specific environment and startup programs

PATH=$PATH:$HOME/.local/bin:$HOME/bin

export PATH
[root@rhel7 ~]#
```

4.3. ~/.bash_login

When **.bash_profile** does not exist, then **bash** will check for ~/**.bash_login** and source it.

Neither Debian nor Red Hat have this file by default.

4.4. ~/.profile

When neither ~/**.bash_profile** and ~/**.bash_login** exist, then bash will verify the existence of ~/**.profile** and execute it. This file does not exist by default on Red Hat.

On Debian this script can execute ~/**.bashrc** and will add $HOME/bin to the $PATH variable.

```
root@debian7:~# tail -11 /home/paul/.profile
if [ -n "$BASH_VERSION" ]; then
    # include .bashrc if it exists
    if [ -f "$HOME/.bashrc" ]; then
        . "$HOME/.bashrc"
    fi
fi

# set PATH so it includes user's private bin if it exists
if [ -d "$HOME/bin" ] ; then
    PATH="$HOME/bin:$PATH"
fi
```

RHEL/CentOS does not have this file by default.

4.5. ~/.bashrc

The ~/**.bashrc** script is often sourced by other scripts. Let us take a look at what it does by default.

Red Hat uses a very simple ~/**.bashrc**, checking for **/etc/bashrc** and sourcing it. It also leaves room for custom aliases and functions.

```
[root@rhel7 ~]# cat /home/paul/.bashrc
# .bashrc

# Source global definitions
if [ -f /etc/bashrc ]; then
        . /etc/bashrc
fi

# Uncomment the following line if you don't like systemctl's auto-paging feature:
# export SYSTEMD_PAGER=

# User specific aliases and functions
```

On Debian this script is quite a bit longer and configures $PS1, some history variables and a number af active and inactive aliases.

```
root@debian7:~# wc -l /home/paul/.bashrc
110 /home/paul/.bashrc
```

4.6. ~/.bash_logout

When exiting **bash**, it can execute ~/.**bash_logout**.

Debian use this opportunity to clear the console screen.

```
serena@deb503:~$ cat .bash_logout
# ~/.bash_logout: executed by bash(1) when login shell exits.

# when leaving the console clear the screen to increase privacy

if [ "$SHLVL" = 1 ]; then
    [ -x /usr/bin/clear_console ] && /usr/bin/clear_console -q
fi
```

Red Hat Enterprise Linux 5 will simple call the **/usr/bin/clear** command in this script.

```
[serena@rhel53 ~]$ cat .bash_logout
# ~/.bash_logout

/usr/bin/clear
```

Red Hat Enterprise Linux 6 and 7 create this file, but leave it empty (except for a comment).

```
paul@rhel65:~$ cat .bash_logout
# ~/.bash_logout
```

4.7. Debian overview

Below is a table overview of when Debian is running any of these bash startup scripts.

Table 4.1. Debian User Environment

script	su	su -	ssh	gdm
~./bashrc	no	yes	yes	yes
~/.profile	no	yes	yes	yes
/etc/profile	no	yes	yes	yes
/etc/bash.bashrc	yes	no	no	yes

4.8. RHEL5 overview

Below is a table overview of when Red Hat Enterprise Linux 5 is running any of these bash startup scripts.

Table 4.2. Red Hat User Environment

script	su	su -	ssh	gdm
~./bashrc	yes	yes	yes	yes
~/.bash_profile	no	yes	yes	yes
/etc/profile	no	yes	yes	yes
/etc/bashrc	yes	yes	yes	yes

4.9. practice: user profiles

1. Make a list of all the profile files on your system.

2. Read the contents of each of these, often they **source** extra scripts.

3. Put a unique variable, alias and function in each of those files.

4. Try several different ways to obtain a shell (su, su -, ssh, tmux, gnome-terminal, Ctrl-alt-F1, ...) and verify which of your custom variables, aliases and function are present in your environment.

5. Do you also know the order in which they are executed?

6. When an application depends on a setting in $HOME/.profile, does it matter whether $HOME/.bash_profile exists or not ?

4.10. solution: user profiles

1. Make a list of all the profile files on your system.

```
ls -a ~ ; ls -l /etc/pro* /etc/bash*
```

2. Read the contents of each of these, often they **source** extra scripts.

3. Put a unique variable, alias and function in each of those files.

4. Try several different ways to obtain a shell (su, su -, ssh, tmux, gnome-terminal, Ctrl-alt-F1, ...) and verify which of your custom variables, aliases and function are present in your environment.

5. Do you also know the order in which they are executed?

```
same name aliases, functions and variables will overwrite each other
```

6. When an application depends on a setting in $HOME/.profile, does it matter whether $HOME/.bash_profile exists or not ?

```
Yes it does matter. (man bash /INVOCATION)
```

Chapter 5. groups

Users can be listed in **groups**. Groups allow you to set permissions on the group level instead of having to set permissions for every individual user.

Every Unix or Linux distribution will have a graphical tool to manage groups. Novice users are advised to use this graphical tool. More experienced users can use command line tools to manage users, but be careful: Some distributions do not allow the mixed use of GUI and CLI tools to manage groups (YaST in Novell Suse). Senior administrators can edit the relevant files directly with **vi** or **vigr**.

5.1. groupadd

Groups can be created with the **groupadd** command. The example below shows the creation of five (empty) groups.

```
root@laika:~# groupadd tennis
root@laika:~# groupadd football
root@laika:~# groupadd snooker
root@laika:~# groupadd formula1
root@laika:~# groupadd salsa
```

5.2. group file

Users can be a member of several groups. Group membership is defined by the **/etc/group** file.

```
root@laika:~# tail -5 /etc/group
tennis:x:1006:
football:x:1007:
snooker:x:1008:
formula1:x:1009:
salsa:x:1010:
root@laika:~#
```

The first field is the group's name. The second field is the group's (encrypted) password (can be empty). The third field is the group identification or **GID**. The fourth field is the list of members, these groups have no members.

5.3. groups

A user can type the **groups** command to see a list of groups where the user belongs to.

```
[harry@RHEL4b ~]$ groups
harry sports
[harry@RHEL4b ~]$
```

5.4. usermod

Group membership can be modified with the useradd or **usermod** command.

```
root@laika:~# usermod -a -G tennis inge
root@laika:~# usermod -a -G tennis katrien
root@laika:~# usermod -a -G salsa katrien
root@laika:~# usermod -a -G snooker sandra
root@laika:~# usermod -a -G formula1 annelies
root@laika:~# tail -5 /etc/group
tennis:x:1006:inge,katrien
football:x:1007:
snooker:x:1008:sandra
formula1:x:1009:annelies
salsa:x:1010:katrien
root@laika:~#
```

Be careful when using **usermod** to add users to groups. By default, the **usermod** command will **remove** the user from every group of which he is a member if the group is not listed in the command! Using the **-a** (append) switch prevents this behaviour.

5.5. groupmod

You can change the group name with the **groupmod** command.

```
root@laika:~# groupmod -n darts snooker
root@laika:~# tail -5 /etc/group
tennis:x:1006:inge,katrien
football:x:1007:
formula1:x:1009:annelies
salsa:x:1010:katrien
darts:x:1008:sandra
```

5.6. groupdel

You can permanently remove a group with the **groupdel** command.

```
root@laika:~# groupdel tennis
root@laika:~#
```

5.7. gpasswd

You can delegate control of group membership to another user with the **gpasswd** command. In the example below we delegate permissions to add and remove group members to serena for the sports group. Then we **su** to serena and add harry to the sports group.

```
[root@RHEL4b ~]# gpasswd -A serena sports
[root@RHEL4b ~]# su - serena
[serena@RHEL4b ~]$ id harry
uid=516(harry) gid=520(harry) groups=520(harry)
[serena@RHEL4b ~]$ gpasswd -a harry sports
Adding user harry to group sports
[serena@RHEL4b ~]$ id harry
uid=516(harry) gid=520(harry) groups=520(harry),522(sports)
[serena@RHEL4b ~]$ tail -1 /etc/group
sports:x:522:serena,venus,harry
[serena@RHEL4b ~]$
```

Group administrators do not have to be a member of the group. They can remove themselves from a group, but this does not influence their ability to add or remove members.

```
[serena@RHEL4b ~]$ gpasswd -d serena sports
Removing user serena from group sports
[serena@RHEL4b ~]$ exit
```

Information about group administrators is kept in the **/etc/gshadow** file.

```
[root@RHEL4b ~]# tail -1 /etc/gshadow
sports:!:serena:venus,harry
[root@RHEL4b ~]#
```

To remove all group administrators from a group, use the **gpasswd** command to set an empty administrators list.

```
[root@RHEL4b ~]# gpasswd -A "" sports
```

5.8. newgrp

You can start a **child shell** with a new temporary **primary group** using the **newgrp** command.

```
root@rhel65:~# mkdir prigroup
root@rhel65:~# cd prigroup/
root@rhel65:~/prigroup# touch standard.txt
root@rhel65:~/prigroup# ls -l
total 0
-rw-r--r--. 1 root root 0 Apr 13 17:49 standard.txt
root@rhel65:~/prigroup# echo $SHLVL
1
root@rhel65:~/prigroup# newgrp tennis
root@rhel65:~/prigroup# echo $SHLVL
2
root@rhel65:~/prigroup# touch newgrp.txt
root@rhel65:~/prigroup# ls -l
total 0
-rw-r--r--. 1 root tennis 0 Apr 13 17:49 newgrp.txt
-rw-r--r--. 1 root root   0 Apr 13 17:49 standard.txt
root@rhel65:~/prigroup# exit
exit
root@rhel65:~/prigroup#
```

5.9. vigr

Similar to vipw, the **vigr** command can be used to manually edit the **/etc/group** file, since it will do proper locking of the file. Only experienced senior administrators should use **vi** or **vigr** to manage groups.

5.10. practice: groups

1. Create the groups tennis, football and sports.

2. In one command, make venus a member of tennis and sports.

3. Rename the football group to foot.

4. Use vi to add serena to the tennis group.

5. Use the id command to verify that serena is a member of tennis.

6. Make someone responsible for managing group membership of foot and sports. Test that it works.

5.11. solution: groups

1. Create the groups tennis, football and sports.

```
groupadd tennis ; groupadd football ; groupadd sports
```

2. In one command, make venus a member of tennis and sports.

```
usermod -a -G tennis,sports venus
```

3. Rename the football group to foot.

```
groupmod -n foot football
```

4. Use vi to add serena to the tennis group.

```
vi /etc/group
```

5. Use the id command to verify that serena is a member of tennis.

```
id (and after logoff logon serena should be member)
```

6. Make someone responsible for managing group membership of foot and sports. Test that it works.

```
gpasswd -A (to make manager)
```

```
gpasswd -a (to add member)
```

Part II. file security

Table of Contents

Chapter 6. standard file permissions

This chapter contains details about basic file security through **file ownership** and **file permissions**.

6.1. file ownership

6.1.1. user owner and group owner

The **users** and **groups** of a system can be locally managed in **/etc/passwd** and **/etc/group**, or they can be in a NIS, LDAP, or Samba domain. These users and groups can **own** files. Actually, every file has a **user owner** and a **group owner**, as can be seen in the following screenshot.

```
paul@rhel65:~/owners$ ls -lh
total 636K
-rw-r--r--. 1 paul snooker 1.1K Apr  8 18:47 data.odt
-rw-r--r--. 1 paul paul    626K Apr  8 18:46 file1
-rw-r--r--. 1 root tennis   185 Apr  8 18:46 file2
-rw-rw-r--. 1 root root       0 Apr  8 18:47 stuff.txt
paul@rhel65:~/owners$
```

User paul owns three files; file1 has paul as **user owner** and has the group paul as **group owner**, data.odt is **group owned** by the group snooker, file2 by the group tennis.

The last file is called stuff.txt and is owned by the root user and the root group.

6.1.2. listing user accounts

You can use the following command to list all local user accounts.

```
paul@debian7~$ cut -d: -f1 /etc/passwd | column
root          ntp           sam           bert          naomi
daemon        mysql         tom           rino          matthias2
bin           paul          wouter        antonio       bram
sys           maarten       robrecht      simon         fabrice
sync          kevin         bilal         sven          chimene
games         yuri          dimitri       wouter2       messagebus
man           william       ahmed         tarik         roger
lp            yves          dylan         jan           frank
mail          kris          robin         ian           toon
news          hamid         matthias      ivan          rinus
uucp          vladimir      ben           azeddine      eddy
proxy         abiy          mike          eric          bram2
www-data      david         kevin2        kamel         keith
backup        chahid        kenzo         ischa         jesse
list          stef          aaron         bart          frederick
irc           joeri         lorenzo       omer          hans
gnats         glenn         jens          kurt          dries
nobody        yannick       ruben         steve         steve2
libuuid       christof      jelle         constantin    tomas
Debian-exim   george        stefaan       sam2          johan
statd         joost         marc          bjorn         tom2
sshd          arno          thomas        ronald
```

6.1.3. chgrp

You can change the group owner of a file using the **chgrp** command.

```
root@rhel65:/home/paul/owners# ls -l file2
-rw-r--r--. 1 root tennis 185 Apr  8 18:46 file2
root@rhel65:/home/paul/owners# chgrp snooker file2
root@rhel65:/home/paul/owners# ls -l file2
-rw-r--r--. 1 root snooker 185 Apr  8 18:46 file2
root@rhel65:/home/paul/owners#
```

6.1.4. chown

The user owner of a file can be changed with **chown** command.

```
root@laika:/home/paul# ls -l FileForPaul
-rw-r--r-- 1 root paul 0 2008-08-06 14:11 FileForPaul
root@laika:/home/paul# chown paul FileForPaul
root@laika:/home/paul# ls -l FileForPaul
-rw-r--r-- 1 paul paul 0 2008-08-06 14:11 FileForPaul
```

You can also use **chown** to change both the user owner and the group owner.

```
root@laika:/home/paul# ls -l FileForPaul
-rw-r--r-- 1 paul paul 0 2008-08-06 14:11 FileForPaul
root@laika:/home/paul# chown root:project42 FileForPaul
root@laika:/home/paul# ls -l FileForPaul
-rw-r--r-- 1 root project42 0 2008-08-06 14:11 FileForPaul
```

6.2. list of special files

When you use **ls -l**, for each file you can see ten characters before the user and group owner. The first character tells us the type of file. Regular files get a -, directories get a **d**, symbolic links are shown with an **l**, pipes get a **p**, character devices a **c**, block devices a **b**, and sockets an **s**.

Table 6.1. Unix special files

first character	file type
-	normal file
d	directory
l	symbolic link
p	named pipe
b	block device
c	character device
s	socket

Below a screenshot of a character device (the console) and a block device (the hard disk).

```
paul@debian6lt~$ ls -ld /dev/console /dev/sda
crw-------   1 root root  5, 1 Mar 15 12:45 /dev/console
brw-rw----   1 root disk  8, 0 Mar 15 12:45 /dev/sda
```

And here you can see a directory, a regular file and a symbolic link.

```
paul@debian6lt~$ ls -ld /etc /etc/hosts /etc/motd
drwxr-xr-x 128 root root 12288 Mar 15 18:34 /etc
-rw-r--r--   1 root root   372 Dec 10 17:36 /etc/hosts
lrwxrwxrwx   1 root root    13 Dec  5 10:36 /etc/motd -> /var/run/motd
```

6.3. permissions

6.3.1. rwx

The nine characters following the file type denote the permissions in three triplets. A permission can be **r** for read access, **w** for write access, and **x** for execute. You need the **r** permission to list (ls) the contents of a directory. You need the **x** permission to enter (cd) a directory. You need the **w** permission to create files in or remove files from a directory.

Table 6.2. standard Unix file permissions

permission	on a file	on a directory
r (read)	read file contents (cat)	read directory contents (ls)
w (write)	change file contents (vi)	create files in (touch)
x (execute)	execute the file	enter the directory (cd)

6.3.2. three sets of rwx

We already know that the output of **ls -l** starts with ten characters for each file. This screenshot shows a regular file (because the first character is a -).

```
paul@RHELv4u4:~/test$ ls -l proc42.bash
-rwxr-xr--  1 paul proj 984 Feb  6 12:01 proc42.bash
```

Below is a table describing the function of all ten characters.

Table 6.3. Unix file permissions position

position	characters	function
1	-	this is a regular file
2-4	rwx	permissions for the **user owner**
5-7	r-x	permissions for the **group owner**
8-10	r--	permissions for **others**

When you are the **user owner** of a file, then the **user owner permissions** apply to you. The rest of the permissions have no influence on your access to the file.

When you belong to the **group** that is the **group owner** of a file, then the **group owner permissions** apply to you. The rest of the permissions have no influence on your access to the file.

When you are not the **user owner** of a file and you do not belong to the **group owner**, then the **others permissions** apply to you. The rest of the permissions have no influence on your access to the file.

6.3.3. permission examples

Some example combinations on files and directories are seen in this screenshot. The name of the file explains the permissions.

```
paul@laika:~/perms$ ls -lh
total 12K
drwxr-xr-x 2 paul paul 4.0K 2007-02-07 22:26 AllEnter_UserCreateDelete
-rwxrwxrwx 1 paul paul    0 2007-02-07 22:21 EveryoneFullControl.txt
-r--r----- 1 paul paul    0 2007-02-07 22:21 OnlyOwnersRead.txt
-rwxrwx--- 1 paul paul    0 2007-02-07 22:21 OwnersAll_RestNothing.txt
dr-xr-x--- 2 paul paul 4.0K 2007-02-07 22:25 UserAndGroupEnter
dr-x------ 2 paul paul 4.0K 2007-02-07 22:25 OnlyUserEnter
paul@laika:~/perms$
```

To summarise, the first **rwx** triplet represents the permissions for the **user owner**. The second triplet corresponds to the **group owner**; it specifies permissions for all members of that group. The third triplet defines permissions for all **other** users that are not the user owner and are not a member of the group owner.

6.3.4. setting permissions (chmod)

Permissions can be changed with **chmod**. The first example gives the user owner execute permissions.

```
paul@laika:~/perms$ ls -l permissions.txt
-rw-r--r-- 1 paul paul 0 2007-02-07 22:34 permissions.txt
paul@laika:~/perms$ chmod u+x permissions.txt
paul@laika:~/perms$ ls -l permissions.txt
-rwxr--r-- 1 paul paul 0 2007-02-07 22:34 permissions.txt
```

This example removes the group owners read permission.

```
paul@laika:~/perms$ chmod g-r permissions.txt
paul@laika:~/perms$ ls -l permissions.txt
-rwx---r-- 1 paul paul 0 2007-02-07 22:34 permissions.txt
```

This example removes the others read permission.

```
paul@laika:~/perms$ chmod o-r permissions.txt
paul@laika:~/perms$ ls -l permissions.txt
-rwx------ 1 paul paul 0 2007-02-07 22:34 permissions.txt
```

This example gives all of them the write permission.

```
paul@laika:~/perms$ chmod a+w permissions.txt
paul@laika:~/perms$ ls -l permissions.txt
-rwx-w--w- 1 paul paul 0 2007-02-07 22:34 permissions.txt
```

You don't even have to type the a.

```
paul@laika:~/perms$ chmod +x permissions.txt
paul@laika:~/perms$ ls -l permissions.txt
-rwx-wx-wx 1 paul paul 0 2007-02-07 22:34 permissions.txt
```

You can also set explicit permissions.

```
paul@laika:~/perms$ chmod u=rw permissions.txt
paul@laika:~/perms$ ls -l permissions.txt
-rw--wx-wx 1 paul paul 0 2007-02-07 22:34 permissions.txt
```

Feel free to make any kind of combination.

```
paul@laika:~/perms$ chmod u=rw,g=rw,o=r permissions.txt
paul@laika:~/perms$ ls -l permissions.txt
-rw-rw-r-- 1 paul paul 0 2007-02-07 22:34 permissions.txt
```

Even fishy combinations are accepted by chmod.

```
paul@laika:~/perms$ chmod u=rwx,ug+rw,o=r permissions.txt
paul@laika:~/perms$ ls -l permissions.txt
-rwxrw-r-- 1 paul paul 0 2007-02-07 22:34 permissions.txt
```

6.3.5. setting octal permissions

Most Unix administrators will use the **old school** octal system to talk about and set permissions. Look at the triplet bitwise, equating r to 4, w to 2, and x to 1.

Table 6.4. Octal permissions

binary	octal	permission
000	0	---
001	1	--x
010	2	-w-
011	3	-wx
100	4	r--
101	5	r-x
110	6	rw-
111	7	rwx

This makes **777** equal to rwxrwxrwx and by the same logic, 654 mean rw-r-xr-- . The **chmod** command will accept these numbers.

```
paul@laika:~/perms$ chmod 777 permissions.txt
paul@laika:~/perms$ ls -l permissions.txt
-rwxrwxrwx 1 paul paul 0 2007-02-07 22:34 permissions.txt
paul@laika:~/perms$ chmod 664 permissions.txt
paul@laika:~/perms$ ls -l permissions.txt
-rw-rw-r-- 1 paul paul 0 2007-02-07 22:34 permissions.txt
paul@laika:~/perms$ chmod 750 permissions.txt
paul@laika:~/perms$ ls -l permissions.txt
-rwxr-x--- 1 paul paul 0 2007-02-07 22:34 permissions.txt
```

6.3.6. umask

When creating a file or directory, a set of default permissions are applied. These default permissions are determined by the **umask**. The **umask** specifies permissions that you do not want set on by default. You can display the **umask** with the **umask** command.

```
[Harry@RHEL4b ~]$ umask
0002
[Harry@RHEL4b ~]$ touch test
[Harry@RHEL4b ~]$ ls -l test
-rw-rw-r--  1 Harry Harry 0 Jul 24 06:03 test
[Harry@RHEL4b ~]$
```

As you can also see, the file is also not executable by default. This is a general security feature among Unixes; newly created files are never executable by default. You have to explicitly do a **chmod +x** to make a file executable. This also means that the 1 bit in the **umask** has no meaning--a **umask** of 0022 is the same as 0033.

6.3.7. mkdir -m

When creating directories with **mkdir** you can use the **-m** option to set the **mode**. This screenshot explains.

```
paul@debian5~$ mkdir -m 700 MyDir
paul@debian5~$ mkdir -m 777 Public
paul@debian5~$ ls -dl MyDir/ Public/
drwx------ 2 paul paul 4096 2011-10-16 19:16 MyDir/
drwxrwxrwx 2 paul paul 4096 2011-10-16 19:16 Public/
```

6.3.8. cp -p

To preserve permissions and time stamps from source files, use **cp -p**.

```
paul@laika:~/perms$ cp file* cp
paul@laika:~/perms$ cp -p file* cpp
paul@laika:~/perms$ ll *
-rwx------ 1 paul paul    0 2008-08-25 13:26 file33
-rwxr-x--- 1 paul paul    0 2008-08-25 13:26 file42

cp:
total 0
-rwx------ 1 paul paul 0 2008-08-25 13:34 file33
-rwxr-x--- 1 paul paul 0 2008-08-25 13:34 file42

cpp:
total 0
-rwx------ 1 paul paul 0 2008-08-25 13:26 file33
-rwxr-x--- 1 paul paul 0 2008-08-25 13:26 file42
```

6.4. practice: standard file permissions

1. As normal user, create a directory ~/permissions. Create a file owned by yourself in there.

2. Copy a file owned by root from /etc/ to your permissions dir, who owns this file now ?

3. As root, create a file in the users ~/permissions directory.

4. As normal user, look at who owns this file created by root.

5. Change the ownership of all files in ~/permissions to yourself.

6. Make sure you have all rights to these files, and others can only read.

7. With chmod, is 770 the same as rwxrwx--- ?

8. With chmod, is 664 the same as r-xr-xr-- ?

9. With chmod, is 400 the same as r-------- ?

10. With chmod, is 734 the same as rwxr-xr-- ?

11a. Display the umask in octal and in symbolic form.

11b. Set the umask to 077, but use the symbolic format to set it. Verify that this works.

12. Create a file as root, give only read to others. Can a normal user read this file ? Test writing to this file with vi.

13a. Create a file as normal user, give only read to others. Can another normal user read this file ? Test writing to this file with vi.

13b. Can root read this file ? Can root write to this file with vi ?

14. Create a directory that belongs to a group, where every member of that group can read and write to files, and create files. Make sure that people can only delete their own files.

6.5. solution: standard file permissions

1. As normal user, create a directory ~/permissions. Create a file owned by yourself in there.

```
mkdir ~/permissions ; touch ~/permissions/myfile.txt
```

2. Copy a file owned by root from /etc/ to your permissions dir, who owns this file now ?

```
cp /etc/hosts ~/permissions/
```

The copy is owned by you.

3. As root, create a file in the users ~/permissions directory.

```
(become root)# touch /home/username/permissions/rootfile
```

4. As normal user, look at who owns this file created by root.

```
ls -l ~/permissions
```

The file created by root is owned by root.

5. Change the ownership of all files in ~/permissions to yourself.

```
chown user ~/permissions/*
```

You cannot become owner of the file that belongs to root.

6. Make sure you have all rights to these files, and others can only read.

```
chmod 644 (on files)
```

```
chmod 755 (on directories)
```

7. With chmod, is 770 the same as rwxrwx--- ?

yes

8. With chmod, is 664 the same as r-xr-xr-- ?

No

9. With chmod, is 400 the same as r-------- ?

yes

10. With chmod, is 734 the same as rwxr-xr-- ?

no

11a. Display the umask in octal and in symbolic form.

```
umask ; umask -S
```

11b. Set the umask to 077, but use the symbolic format to set it. Verify that this works.

```
umask -S u=rwx,go=
```

12. Create a file as root, give only read to others. Can a normal user read this file ? Test writing to this file with vi.

```
(become root)

# echo hello > /home/username/root.txt

# chmod 744 /home/username/root.txt

(become user)

vi ~/root.txt
```

13a. Create a file as normal user, give only read to others. Can another normal user read this file ? Test writing to this file with vi.

```
echo hello > file ; chmod 744 file
```

Yes, others can read this file

13b. Can root read this file ? Can root write to this file with vi ?

Yes, root can read and write to this file. Permissions do not apply to root.

14. Create a directory that belongs to a group, where every member of that group can read and write to files, and create files. Make sure that people can only delete their own files.

```
mkdir /home/project42 ; groupadd project42

chgrp project42 /home/project42 ; chmod 775 /home/project42
```

You can not yet do the last part of this exercise...

Chapter 7. advanced file permissions

7.1. sticky bit on directory

You can set the **sticky bit** on a directory to prevent users from removing files that they do not own as a user owner. The sticky bit is displayed at the same location as the x permission for others. The sticky bit is represented by a **t** (meaning x is also there) or a **T** (when there is no x for others).

```
root@RHELv4u4:~# mkdir /project55
root@RHELv4u4:~# ls -ld /project55
drwxr-xr-x  2 root root 4096 Feb  7 17:38 /project55
root@RHELv4u4:~# chmod +t /project55/
root@RHELv4u4:~# ls -ld /project55
drwxr-xr-t  2 root root 4096 Feb  7 17:38 /project55
root@RHELv4u4:~#
```

The **sticky bit** can also be set with octal permissions, it is binary 1 in the first of four triplets.

```
root@RHELv4u4:~# chmod 1775 /project55/
root@RHELv4u4:~# ls -ld /project55
drwxrwxr-t  2 root root 4096 Feb  7 17:38 /project55
root@RHELv4u4:~#
```

You will typically find the **sticky bit** on the **/tmp** directory.

```
root@barry:~# ls -ld /tmp
drwxrwxrwt 6 root root 4096 2009-06-04 19:02 /tmp
```

7.2. setgid bit on directory

setgid can be used on directories to make sure that all files inside the directory are owned by the group owner of the directory. The **setgid** bit is displayed at the same location as the x permission for group owner. The **setgid** bit is represented by an **s** (meaning x is also there) or a **S** (when there is no x for the group owner). As this example shows, even though **root** does not belong to the group proj55, the files created by root in /project55 will belong to proj55 since the **setgid** is set.

```
root@RHELv4u4:~# groupadd proj55
root@RHELv4u4:~# chown root:proj55 /project55/
root@RHELv4u4:~# chmod 2775 /project55/
root@RHELv4u4:~# touch /project55/fromroot.txt
root@RHELv4u4:~# ls -ld /project55/
drwxrwsr-x  2 root proj55 4096 Feb  7 17:45 /project55/
root@RHELv4u4:~# ls -l /project55/
total 4
-rw-r--r--  1 root proj55 0 Feb  7 17:45 fromroot.txt
root@RHELv4u4:~#
```

You can use the **find** command to find all **setgid** directories.

```
paul@laika:~$ find / -type d -perm -2000 2> /dev/null
/var/log/mysql
/var/log/news
/var/local
...
```

7.3. setgid and setuid on regular files

These two permissions cause an executable file to be executed with the permissions of the **file owner** instead of the **executing owner**. This means that if any user executes a program that belongs to the **root user**, and the **setuid** bit is set on that program, then the program runs as **root**. This can be dangerous, but sometimes this is good for security.

Take the example of passwords; they are stored in **/etc/shadow** which is only readable by **root**. (The **root** user never needs permissions anyway.)

```
root@RHELv4u4:~# ls -l /etc/shadow
-r--------  1 root root 1260 Jan 21 07:49 /etc/shadow
```

Changing your password requires an update of this file, so how can normal non-root users do this? Let's take a look at the permissions on the **/usr/bin/passwd**.

```
root@RHELv4u4:~# ls -l /usr/bin/passwd
-r-s--x--x  1 root root 21200 Jun 17  2005 /usr/bin/passwd
```

When running the **passwd** program, you are executing it with **root** credentials.

You can use the **find** command to find all **setuid** programs.

```
paul@laika:~$ find /usr/bin -type f -perm -04000
/usr/bin/arping
/usr/bin/kgrantpty
/usr/bin/newgrp
/usr/bin/chfn
/usr/bin/sudo
/usr/bin/fping6
/usr/bin/passwd
/usr/bin/gpasswd
...
```

In most cases, setting the **setuid** bit on executables is sufficient. Setting the **setgid** bit will result in these programs to run with the credentials of their group owner.

7.4. setuid on sudo

The **sudo** binary has the **setuid** bit set, so any user can run it with the effective userid of root.

```
paul@rhel65:~$ ls -l $(which sudo)
---s--x--x. 1 root root 123832 Oct  7  2013 /usr/bin/sudo
paul@rhel65:~$
```

7.5. practice: sticky, setuid and setgid bits

1a. Set up a directory, owned by the group sports.

1b. Members of the sports group should be able to create files in this directory.

1c. All files created in this directory should be group-owned by the sports group.

1d. Users should be able to delete only their own user-owned files.

1e. Test that this works!

2. Verify the permissions on **/usr/bin/passwd**. Remove the **setuid**, then try changing your password as a normal user. Reset the permissions back and try again.

3. If time permits (or if you are waiting for other students to finish this practice), read about file attributes in the man page of chattr and lsattr. Try setting the i attribute on a file and test that it works.

7.6. solution: sticky, setuid and setgid bits

1a. Set up a directory, owned by the group sports.

```
groupadd sports

mkdir /home/sports

chown root:sports /home/sports
```

1b. Members of the sports group should be able to create files in this directory.

```
chmod 770 /home/sports
```

1c. All files created in this directory should be group-owned by the sports group.

```
chmod 2770 /home/sports
```

1d. Users should be able to delete only their own user-owned files.

```
chmod +t /home/sports
```

1e. Test that this works!

Log in with different users (group members and others and root), create files and watch the permissions. Try changing and deleting files...

2. Verify the permissions on **/usr/bin/passwd**. Remove the **setuid**, then try changing your password as a normal user. Reset the permissions back and try again.

```
root@deb503:~# ls -l /usr/bin/passwd
-rwsr-xr-x 1 root root 31704 2009-11-14 15:41 /usr/bin/passwd
root@deb503:~# chmod 755 /usr/bin/passwd
root@deb503:~# ls -l /usr/bin/passwd
-rwxr-xr-x 1 root root 31704 2009-11-14 15:41 /usr/bin/passwd
```

A normal user cannot change password now.

```
root@deb503:~# chmod 4755 /usr/bin/passwd
root@deb503:~# ls -l /usr/bin/passwd
-rwsr-xr-x 1 root root 31704 2009-11-14 15:41 /usr/bin/passwd
```

3. If time permits (or if you are waiting for other students to finish this practice), read about file attributes in the man page of chattr and lsattr. Try setting the i attribute on a file and test that it works.

```
paul@laika:~$ sudo su -
[sudo] password for paul:
root@laika:~# mkdir attr
root@laika:~# cd attr/
root@laika:~/attr# touch file42
root@laika:~/attr# lsattr
----------------- ./file42
root@laika:~/attr# chattr +i file42
```

```
root@laika:~/attr# lsattr
----i------------- ./file42
root@laika:~/attr# rm -rf file42
rm: cannot remove `file42': Operation not permitted
root@laika:~/attr# chattr -i file42
root@laika:~/attr# rm -rf file42
root@laika:~/attr#
```

Chapter 8. access control lists

Standard Unix permissions might not be enough for some organisations. This chapter introduces **access control lists** or **acl's** to further protect files and directories.

8.1. acl in /etc/fstab

File systems that support **access control lists**, or **acls**, have to be mounted with the **acl** option listed in **/etc/fstab**. In the example below, you can see that the root file system has **acl** support, whereas /home/data does not.

```
root@laika:~# tail -4 /etc/fstab
/dev/sda1           /               ext3    acl,relatime    0   1
/dev/sdb2           /home/data      auto    noacl,defaults  0   0
pasha:/home/r       /home/pasha     nfs     defaults        0   0
wolf:/srv/data      /home/wolf      nfs     defaults        0   0
```

8.2. getfacl

Reading **acls** can be done with **/usr/bin/getfacl**. This screenshot shows how to read the **acl** of **file33** with **getfacl**.

```
paul@laika:~/test$ getfacl file33
# file: file33
# owner: paul
# group: paul
user::rw-
group::r--
mask::rwx
other::r--
```

8.3. setfacl

Writing or changing **acls** can be done with **/usr/bin/setfacl**. These screenshots show how to change the **acl** of **file33** with **setfacl**.

First we add **u**ser **sandra** with octal permission **7** to the **acl**.

```
paul@laika:~/test$ setfacl -m u:sandra:7 file33
```

Then we add the **group tennis** with octal permission **6** to the **acl** of the same file.

```
paul@laika:~/test$ setfacl -m g:tennis:6 file33
```

The result is visible with **getfacl**.

```
paul@laika:~/test$ getfacl file33
# file: file33
# owner: paul
# group: paul
user::rw-
user:sandra:rwx
group::r--
group:tennis:rw-
mask::rwx
other::r--
```

8.4. remove an acl entry

The **-x** option of the **setfacl** command will remove an **acl** entry from the targeted file.

```
paul@laika:~/test$ setfacl -m u:sandra:7 file33
paul@laika:~/test$ getfacl file33 | grep sandra
user:sandra:rwx
paul@laika:~/test$ setfacl -x sandra file33
paul@laika:~/test$ getfacl file33 | grep sandra
```

Note that omitting the **u** or **g** when defining the **acl** for an account will default it to a user account.

8.5. remove the complete acl

The **-b** option of the **setfacl** command will remove the **acl** from the targeted file.

```
paul@laika:~/test$ setfacl -b file33
paul@laika:~/test$ getfacl file33
# file: file33
# owner: paul
# group: paul
user::rw-
group::r--
other::r--
```

8.6. the acl mask

The **acl mask** defines the maximum effective permissions for any entry in the **acl**. This **mask** is calculated every time you execute the **setfacl** or **chmod** commands.

You can prevent the calculation by using the **--no-mask** switch.

```
paul@laika:~/test$ setfacl --no-mask -m u:sandra:7 file33
paul@laika:~/test$ getfacl file33
# file: file33
# owner: paul
# group: paul
user::rw-
user:sandra:rwx    #effective:rw-
group::r--
mask::rw-
other::r--
```

8.7. eiciel

Desktop users might want to use **eiciel** to manage **acls** with a graphical tool.

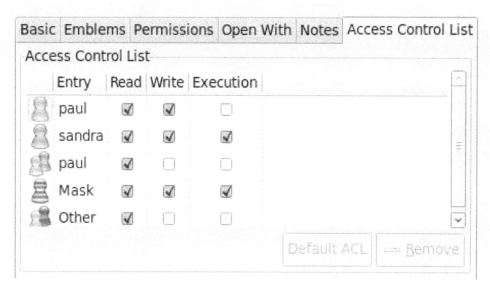

You will need to install **eiciel** and **nautilus-actions** to have an extra tab in **nautilus** to manage **acls**.

```
paul@laika:~$ sudo aptitude install eiciel nautilus-actions
```

Chapter 9. file links

An average computer using Linux has a file system with many **hard links** and **symbolic links**.

To understand links in a file system, you first have to understand what an **inode** is.

9.1. inodes

9.1.1. inode contents

An **inode** is a data structure that contains metadata about a file. When the file system stores a new file on the hard disk, it stores not only the contents (data) of the file, but also extra properties like the name of the file, the creation date, its permissions, the owner of the file, and more. All this information (except the name of the file and the contents of the file) is stored in the **inode** of the file.

The **ls -l** command will display some of the inode contents, as seen in this screenshot.

```
root@rhel53 ~# ls -ld /home/project42/
drwxr-xr-x 4 root pro42 4.0K Mar 27 14:29 /home/project42/
```

9.1.2. inode table

The **inode table** contains all of the **inodes** and is created when you create the file system (with **mkfs**). You can use the **df -i** command to see how many **inodes** are used and free on mounted file systems.

```
root@rhel53 ~# df -i
Filesystem            Inodes   IUsed   IFree IUse% Mounted on
/dev/mapper/VolGroup00-LogVol00
                     4947968  115326 4832642    3% /
/dev/hda1              26104      45   26059    1% /boot
tmpfs                 64417       1   64416    1% /dev/shm
/dev/sda1            262144    2207  259937    1% /home/project42
/dev/sdb1             74400    5519   68881    8% /home/project33
/dev/sdb5                 0       0       0    -  /home/sales
/dev/sdb6            100744      11  100733    1% /home/research
```

In the **df -i** screenshot above you can see the **inode** usage for several mounted **file systems**. You don't see numbers for **/dev/sdb5** because it is a **fat** file system.

9.1.3. inode number

Each **inode** has a unique number (the inode number). You can see the **inode** numbers with the **ls -li** command.

```
paul@RHELv4u4:~/test$ touch file1
paul@RHELv4u4:~/test$ touch file2
paul@RHELv4u4:~/test$ touch file3
paul@RHELv4u4:~/test$ ls -li
total 12
817266 -rw-rw-r-- 1 paul paul 0 Feb  5 15:38 file1
817267 -rw-rw-r-- 1 paul paul 0 Feb  5 15:38 file2
817268 -rw-rw-r-- 1 paul paul 0 Feb  5 15:38 file3
paul@RHELv4u4:~/test$
```

These three files were created one after the other and got three different **inodes** (the first column). All the information you see with this **ls** command resides in the **inode**, except for the filename (which is contained in the directory).

9.1.4. inode and file contents

Let's put some data in one of the files.

```
paul@RHELv4u4:~/test$ ls -li
total 16
817266 -rw-rw-r--  1 paul paul  0 Feb  5 15:38 file1
817270 -rw-rw-r--  1 paul paul 92 Feb  5 15:42 file2
817268 -rw-rw-r--  1 paul paul  0 Feb  5 15:38 file3
paul@RHELv4u4:~/test$ cat file2
It is winter now and it is very cold.
We do not like the cold, we prefer hot summer nights.
paul@RHELv4u4:~/test$
```

The data that is displayed by the **cat** command is not in the **inode**, but somewhere else on the disk. The **inode** contains a pointer to that data.

9.2. about directories

9.2.1. a directory is a table

A **directory** is a special kind of file that contains a table which maps filenames to inodes. Listing our current directory with **ls -ali** will display the contents of the directory file.

```
paul@RHELv4u4:~/test$ ls -ali
total 32
817262 drwxrwxr-x   2 paul paul 4096 Feb  5 15:42 .
800768 drwx------  16 paul paul 4096 Feb  5 15:42 ..
817266 -rw-rw-r--   1 paul paul    0 Feb  5 15:38 file1
817270 -rw-rw-r--   1 paul paul   92 Feb  5 15:42 file2
817268 -rw-rw-r--   1 paul paul    0 Feb  5 15:38 file3
paul@RHELv4u4:~/test$
```

9.2.2. . and ..

You can see five names, and the mapping to their five inodes. The dot **.** is a mapping to itself, and the dotdot **..** is a mapping to the parent directory. The three other names are mappings to different inodes.

9.3. hard links

9.3.1. creating hard links

When we create a **hard link** to a file with **ln**, an extra entry is added in the directory. A new file name is mapped to an existing inode.

```
paul@RHELv4u4:~/test$ ln file2 hardlink_to_file2
paul@RHELv4u4:~/test$ ls -li
total 24
817266 -rw-rw-r--  1 paul paul  0 Feb  5 15:38 file1
817270 -rw-rw-r--  2 paul paul 92 Feb  5 15:42 file2
817268 -rw-rw-r--  1 paul paul  0 Feb  5 15:38 file3
817270 -rw-rw-r--  2 paul paul 92 Feb  5 15:42 hardlink_to_file2
paul@RHELv4u4:~/test$
```

Both files have the same inode, so they will always have the same permissions and the same owner. Both files will have the same content. Actually, both files are equal now, meaning you can safely remove the original file, the hardlinked file will remain. The inode contains a counter, counting the number of hard links to itself. When the counter drops to zero, then the inode is emptied.

9.3.2. finding hard links

You can use the **find** command to look for files with a certain inode. The screenshot below shows how to search for all filenames that point to **inode** 817270. Remember that an **inode** number is unique to its partition.

```
paul@RHELv4u4:~/test$ find / -inum 817270 2> /dev/null
/home/paul/test/file2
/home/paul/test/hardlink_to_file2
```

9.4. symbolic links

Symbolic links (sometimes called **soft links**) do not link to inodes, but create a name to name mapping. Symbolic links are created with **ln -s**. As you can see below, the **symbolic link** gets an inode of its own.

```
paul@RHELv4u4:~/test$ ln -s file2 symlink_to_file2
paul@RHELv4u4:~/test$ ls -li
total 32
817273 -rw-rw-r--  1 paul paul  13 Feb  5 17:06 file1
817270 -rw-rw-r--  2 paul paul 106 Feb  5 17:04 file2
817268 -rw-rw-r--  1 paul paul   0 Feb  5 15:38 file3
817270 -rw-rw-r--  2 paul paul 106 Feb  5 17:04 hardlink_to_file2
817267 lrwxrwxrwx  1 paul paul   5 Feb  5 16:55 symlink_to_file2 -> file2
paul@RHELv4u4:~/test$
```

Permissions on a symbolic link have no meaning, since the permissions of the target apply. Hard links are limited to their own partition (because they point to an inode), symbolic links can link anywhere (other file systems, even networked).

9.5. removing links

Links can be removed with **rm**.

```
paul@laika:~$ touch data.txt
paul@laika:~$ ln -s data.txt sl_data.txt
paul@laika:~$ ln data.txt hl_data.txt
paul@laika:~$ rm sl_data.txt
paul@laika:~$ rm hl_data.txt
```

9.6. practice : links

1. Create two files named winter.txt and summer.txt, put some text in them.

2. Create a hard link to winter.txt named hlwinter.txt.

3. Display the inode numbers of these three files, the hard links should have the same inode.

4. Use the find command to list the two hardlinked files

5. Everything about a file is in the inode, except two things : name them!

6. Create a symbolic link to summer.txt called slsummer.txt.

7. Find all files with inode number 2. What does this information tell you ?

8. Look at the directories /etc/init.d/ /etc/rc2.d/ /etc/rc3.d/ ... do you see the links ?

9. Look in /lib with ls -l...

10. Use **find** to look in your home directory for regular files that do not(!) have one hard link.

9.7. solution : links

1. Create two files named winter.txt and summer.txt, put some text in them.

```
echo cold > winter.txt ; echo hot > summer.txt
```

2. Create a hard link to winter.txt named hlwinter.txt.

```
ln winter.txt hlwinter.txt
```

3. Display the inode numbers of these three files, the hard links should have the same inode.

```
ls -li winter.txt summer.txt hlwinter.txt
```

4. Use the find command to list the two hardlinked files

```
find . -inum xyz #replace xyz with the inode number
```

5. Everything about a file is in the inode, except two things : name them!

The name of the file is in a directory, and the contents is somewhere on the disk.

6. Create a symbolic link to summer.txt called slsummer.txt.

```
ln -s summer.txt slsummer.txt
```

7. Find all files with inode number 2. What does this information tell you ?

It tells you there is more than one inode table (one for every formatted partition + virtual file systems)

8. Look at the directories /etc/init.d/ /etc/rc.d/ /etc/rc3.d/ ... do you see the links ?

```
ls -l /etc/init.d
ls -l /etc/rc2.d
ls -l /etc/rc3.d
```

9. Look in /lib with ls -l...

```
ls -l /lib
```

10. Use **find** to look in your home directory for regular files that do not(!) have one hard link.

```
find ~ ! -links 1 -type f
```

Part III. iptables firewall

Table of Contents

Chapter 10. introduction to routers

What follows is a very brief introduction to using Linux as a router.

10.1. router or firewall

A **router** is a device that connects two networks. A **firewall** is a device that besides acting as a **router**, also contains (and implements) rules to determine whether packets are allowed to travel from one network to another. A firewall can be configured to block access based on networks, hosts, protocols and ports. Firewalls can also change the contents of packets while forwarding them.

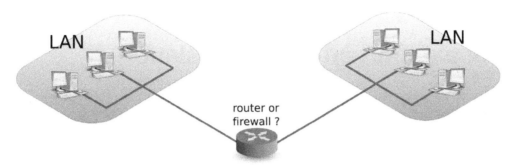

10.2. packet forwarding

Packet forwarding means allowing packets to go from one network to another. When a multihomed host is connected to two different networks, and it allows packets to travel from one network to another through its two network interfaces, it is said to have enabled **packet forwarding**.

10.3. packet filtering

Packet filtering is very similar to packet forwarding, but every packet is individually tested against rules that decide on allowing or dropping the packet. The rules are stored by iptables.

10.4. stateful

A **stateful** firewall is an advancement over stateless firewalls that inspect every individual packet. A stateful firewall will keep a table of active connections, and is knowledgeable enough to recognise when new connections are part of an active session. Linux iptables is a stateful firewall.

10.5. nat (network address translation)

A **nat** device is a router that is also changing the source and/or target ip-address in packets. It is typically used to connect multiple computers in a private address range (rfc 1918) with the (public) internet. A **nat** can hide private addresses from the internet.

It is important to understand that people and vendors do not always use the right term when referring to a certain type of **nat**. Be sure you talk about the same thing. We can distuinguish several types of **nat**.

10.6. pat (port address translation)

nat often includes **pat**. A **pat** device is a router that is also changing the source and/or target tcp/udp port in packets. **pat** is Cisco terminology and is used by **snat, dnat, masquerading** and **port forwarding** in Linux. RFC 3022 calls it **NAPT** and defines the **nat/pat** combo as "traditional nat". A device sold to you as a nat-device will probably do **nat** and **pat**.

10.7. snat (source nat)

A **snat** device is changing the source ip-address when a packet passes our **nat**. **snat** configuration with iptables includes a fixed target source address.

10.8. masquerading

Masquerading is a form of **snat** that will hide the (private) source ip-addresses of your private network using a public ip-address. Masquerading is common on dynamic internet interfaces (broadband modem/routers). Masquerade configuration with iptables uses a dynamic target source address.

10.9. dnat (destination nat)

A **dnat** device is changing the destination ip-address when a packet passes our **nat**.

10.10. port forwarding

When static **dnat** is set up in a way that allows outside connections to enter our private network, then we call it **port forwarding**.

10.11. /proc/sys/net/ipv4/ip_forward

Whether a host is forwarding packets is defined in **/proc/sys/net/ipv4/ip_forward**. The following screenshot shows how to enable packet forwarding on Linux.

```
root@router~# echo 1 > /proc/sys/net/ipv4/ip_forward
```

The next command shows how to disable packet forwarding.

```
root@router~# echo 0 > /proc/sys/net/ipv4/ip_forward
```

Use cat to check if packet forwarding is enabled.

```
root@router~# cat /proc/sys/net/ipv4/ip_forward
```

10.12. /etc/sysctl.conf

By default, most Linux computers are not configured for automatic packet forwarding. To enable packet forwarding whenever the system starts, change the **net.ipv4.ip_forward** variable in **/etc/sysctl.conf** to the value 1.

```
root@router~# grep ip_forward /etc/sysctl.conf
net.ipv4.ip_forward = 0
```

10.13. sysctl

For more information, take a look at the man page of **sysctl**.

```
root@debian6~# man sysctl
root@debian6~# sysctl -a 2>/dev/null | grep ip_forward
net.ipv4.ip_forward = 0
```

10.14. practice: packet forwarding

0. You have the option to select (or create) an internal network when adding a network card in **VirtualBox** or **VMWare**. Use this option to create two internal networks. I named them **leftnet** and **rightnet**, but you can choose any other name.

> **Network**
>
> Adapter 1: Intel PRO/1000 MT Desktop (Bridged Adapter, en1: AirPort)
> Adapter 2: Intel PRO/1000 MT Desktop (Internal Network, 'leftnet')
> Adapter 3: Intel PRO/1000 MT Desktop (Internal Network, 'rightnet')

1. Set up two Linux machines, one on **leftnet**, the other on **rightnet**. Make sure they both get an ip-address in the correct subnet. These two machines will be 'left' and 'right' from the 'router'.

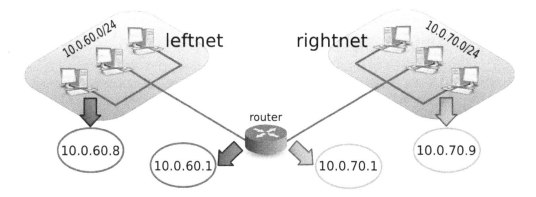

2. Set up a third Linux computer with three network cards, one on **leftnet**, the other on **rightnet**. This computer will be the 'router'. Complete the table below with the relevant names, ip-addresses and **mac-addresses**.

Table 10.1. Packet Forwarding Exercise

	leftnet computer	the router		rightnet computer
MAC				
IP				

3. How can you verify whether the **router** will allow packet forwarding by default or not ? Test that you can **ping** from the **router** to the two other machines, and from those two machines to the **router**. Use **arp -a** to make sure you are connected with the correct **mac addresses**.

4. **Ping** from the leftnet computer to the rightnet computer. Enable and/or disable packet forwarding on the **router** and verify what happens to the ping between the two networks. If you do not succeed in pinging between the two networks (on different subnets), then use a sniffer like **wireshark** or **tcpdump** to discover the problem.

5. Use **wireshark** or **tcpdump** -xx to answer the following questions. Does the source MAC change when a packet passes through the filter ? And the destination MAC ? What about source and destination IP-addresses ?

6. Remember the third network card on the router ? Connect this card to a LAN with internet connection. On many LAN's the command **dhclient eth0** just works (replace **eth0** with the correct interface).

```
root@router~# dhclient eth0
```

You now have a setup similar to this picture. What needs to be done to give internet access to **leftnet** and **rightnet**.

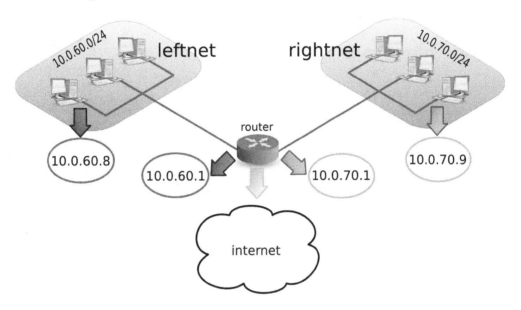

10.15. solution: packet forwarding

Network

Adapter 1: Intel PRO/1000 MT Desktop (Bridged Adapter, en1: AirPort)
Adapter 2: Intel PRO/1000 MT Desktop (Internal Network, 'leftnet')
Adapter 3: Intel PRO/1000 MT Desktop (Internal Network, 'rightnet')

1. Set up two Linux machines, one on **leftnet**, the other on **rightnet**. Make sure they both get an ip-address in the correct subnet. These two machines will be 'left' and 'right' from the 'router'.

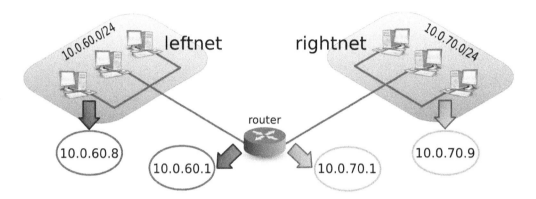

The ip configuration on your computers should be similar to the following two screenshots. Both machines must be in a different subnet (here 192.168.60.0/24 and 192.168.70.0/24). I created a little script on both machines to configure the interfaces.

```
root@left~# cat leftnet.sh
pkill dhclient
ifconfig eth0 192.168.60.8 netmask 255.255.255.0

root@right~# cat rightnet.sh
pkill dhclient
ifconfig eth0 192.168.70.9 netmask 255.255.255.0
```

2. Set up a third Linux computer with three network cards, one on **leftnet**, the other on **rightnet**. This computer will be the 'router'. Complete the table below with the relevant names, ip-addresses and mac-addresses.

```
root@router~# cat router.sh
ifconfig eth1 192.168.60.1 netmask 255.255.255.0
ifconfig eth2 192.168.70.1 netmask 255.255.255.0
#echo 1 > /proc/sys/net/ipv4/ip_forward
```

Your setup may use different ip and mac addresses than the ones in the table below.

Table 10.2. Packet Forwarding Solution

leftnet computer	the router		rightnet computer
08:00:27:f6:ab:b9	08:00:27:43:1f:5a	08:00:27:be:4a:6b	08:00:27:14:8b:17
192.168.60.8	192.168.60.1	192.168.70.1	192.168.70.9

3. How can you verify whether the **router** will allow packet forwarding by default or not ? Test that you can ping from the **router** to the two other machines, and from those two machines to the **router**. Use **arp -a** to make sure you are connected with the correct **mac addresses**.

This can be done with "**grep ip_forward /etc/sysctl.conf**" (1 is enabled, 0 is disabled) or with **sysctl -a | grep ip_for**.

```
root@router~# grep ip_for /etc/sysctl.conf
net.ipv4.ip_forward = 0
```

4. Ping from the leftnet computer to the rightnet computer. Enable and/or disable packet forwarding on the **router** and verify what happens to the ping between the two networks. If you do not succeed in pinging between the two networks (on different subnets), then use a sniffer like wireshark or tcpdump to discover the problem.

Did you forget to add a **default gateway** to the LAN machines ? Use **route add default gw 'ip-address'**.

```
root@left~# route add default gw 192.168.60.1
```

```
root@right~# route add default gw 192.168.70.1
```

You should be able to ping when packet forwarding is enabled (and both default gateways are properly configured). The ping will not work when packet forwarding is disabled or when gateways are not configured correctly.

5. Use wireshark or tcpdump -xx to answer the following questions. Does the source MAC change when a packet passes through the filter ? And the destination MAC ? What about source and destination IP-addresses ?

Both MAC addresses are changed when passing the router. Use **tcpdump -xx** like this:

```
root@router~# tcpdump -xx -i eth1
```

```
root@router~# tcpdump -xx -i eth2
```

6. Remember the third network card on the router ? Connect this card to a LAN with internet connection. On many LAN's the command **dhclient eth0** just works (replace **eth0** with the correct interface.

```
root@router~# dhclient eth0
```

You now have a setup similar to this picture. What needs to be done to give internet access to **leftnet** and **rightnet**.

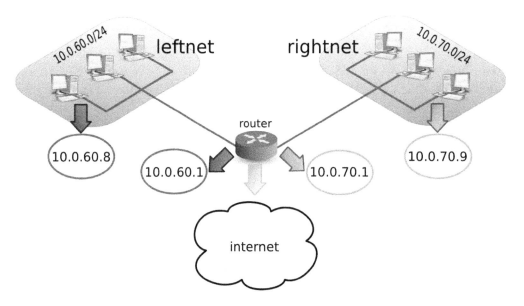

The clients on **leftnet** and **rightnet** need a working **dns server**. We use one of Google's dns servers here.

```
echo nameserver 8.8.8.8 > /etc/resolv.conf
```

Chapter 11. iptables firewall

This chapter introduces some simple firewall rules and how to configure them with **iptables**.

iptables is an application that allows a user to configure the firewall functionality built into the **Linux** kernel.

11.1. iptables tables

By default there are three **tables** in the kernel that contain sets of rules.

The **filter table** is used for packet filtering.

```
root@debian6~# iptables -t filter -L
Chain INPUT (policy ACCEPT)
target     prot opt source               destination

Chain FORWARD (policy ACCEPT)
target     prot opt source               destination

Chain OUTPUT (policy ACCEPT)
target     prot opt source               destination
```

The **nat table** is used for address translation.

```
root@debian6~# iptables -t nat -L
Chain PREROUTING (policy ACCEPT)
target     prot opt source               destination

Chain POSTROUTING (policy ACCEPT)
target     prot opt source               destination

Chain OUTPUT (policy ACCEPT)
target     prot opt source               destination
```

The **mangle table** can be used for special-purpose processing of packets.

Series of rules in each table are called a **chain**. We will discuss chains and the nat table later in this chapter.

11.2. starting and stopping iptables

The following screenshot shows how to stop and start **iptables** on Red Hat/Fedora/CentOS and compatible distributions.

```
[root@centos6 ~]# service iptables stop
[root@centos6 ~]# service iptables start
iptables: Applying firewall rules                           [ ok ]
[root@centos6 ~]#
```

Debian and *buntu distributions do not have this script, but allow for an uninstall.

```
root@debian6~# aptitude purge iptables
```

11.3. the filter table

11.3.1. about packet filtering

Packet filtering is a bit more than **packet forwarding**. While **packet forwarding** uses only a routing table to make decisions, **packet filtering** also uses a list of rules. The kernel will inspect packets and decide based on these rules what to do with each packet.

11.3.2. filter table

The filter table in **iptables** has three chains (sets of rules). The INPUT chain is used for any packet coming into the system. The OUTPUT chain is for any packet leaving the system. And the FORWARD chain is for packets that are forwarded (routed) through the system.

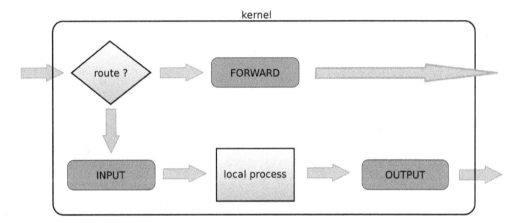

The screenshot below shows how to list the filter table and all its rules.

```
[root@RHEL5 ~]# iptables -t filter -nL
Chain INPUT (policy ACCEPT)
target     prot opt source               destination

Chain FORWARD (policy ACCEPT)
target     prot opt source               destination

Chain OUTPUT (policy ACCEPT)
target     prot opt source               destination
[root@RHEL5 ~]#
```

As you can see, all three chains in the filter table are set to ACCEPT everything. ACCEPT is the default behaviour.

11.3.3. setting default rules

The default for the default rule is indeed to ACCEPT everything. This is not the most secure firewall.

A more secure setup would be to DROP everything. A package that is **dropped** will not continue in any chain, and no warning or error will be sent anywhere.

The below commands lock down a computer. Do not execute these commands inside a remote ssh shell.

```
root@debianpaul~# iptables -P INPUT DROP
root@debianpaul~# iptables -P OUTPUT DROP
root@debianpaul~# iptables -P FORWARD DROP
root@debianpaul~# iptables -L
Chain INPUT (policy DROP)
target     prot opt source               destination

Chain FORWARD (policy DROP)
target     prot opt source               destination

Chain OUTPUT (policy DROP)
target     prot opt source               destination
```

11.3.4. changing policy rules

To start, let's set the default policy for all three chains to drop everything. Note that you might lose your connection when typing this over ssh ;-).

```
[root@RHEL5 ~]# iptables -P INPUT DROP
[root@RHEL5 ~]# iptables -P FORWARD DROP
[root@RHEL5 ~]# iptables -P OUTPUT DROP
```

Next, we allow the server to use its own loopback device (this allows the server to access its services running on localhost). We first append a rule to the INPUT chain to allow (ACCEPT) traffic from the lo (loopback) interface, then we do the same to allow packets to leave the system through the loopback interface.

```
[root@RHEL5 ~]# iptables -A INPUT -i lo -j ACCEPT
[root@RHEL5 ~]# iptables -A OUTPUT -o lo -j ACCEPT
```

Looking at the filter table again (omitting -t filter because it is the default table).

```
[root@RHEL5 ~]# iptables -nL
Chain INPUT (policy DROP)
target     prot opt source               destination
ACCEPT     all  --  0.0.0.0/0            0.0.0.0/0

Chain FORWARD (policy DROP)
target     prot opt source               destination

Chain OUTPUT (policy DROP)
target     prot opt source               destination
ACCEPT     all  --  0.0.0.0/0            0.0.0.0/0
```

11.3.5. Allowing ssh over eth0

This example show how to add two rules to allow ssh access to your system from outside.

```
[root@RHEL5 ~]# iptables -A INPUT -i eth0 -p tcp --dport 22 -j ACCEPT
[root@RHEL5 ~]# iptables -A OUTPUT -o eth0 -p tcp --sport 22 -j ACCEPT
```

The filter table will look something like this screenshot (note that -v is added for more verbose output).

```
[root@RHEL5 ~]# iptables -nvL
Chain INPUT (policy DROP 7 packets, 609 bytes)
 pkts bytes target prot opt in    out   source      destination
    0     0 ACCEPT all  --  lo    *     0.0.0.0/0   0.0.0.0/0
    0     0 ACCEPT tcp  --  eth0  *     0.0.0.0/0   0.0.0.0/0   tcp dpt:22

Chain FORWARD (policy DROP 0 packets, 0 bytes)
 pkts bytes target prot opt in    out   source      destination

Chain OUTPUT (policy DROP 3 packets, 228 bytes)
 pkts bytes target prot opt in    out   source      destination
    0     0 ACCEPT all  --  *     lo    0.0.0.0/0   0.0.0.0/0
    0     0 ACCEPT tcp  --  *     eth0  0.0.0.0/0   0.0.0.0/0   tcp spt:22
[root@RHEL5 ~]#
```

11.3.6. Allowing access from a subnet

This example shows how to allow access from any computer in the 10.1.1.0/24 network, but only through eth1. There is no port (application) limitation here.

```
[root@RHEL5 ~]# iptables -A INPUT -i eth1 -s 10.1.1.0/24 -p tcp -j ACCEPT
[root@RHEL5 ~]# iptables -A OUTPUT -o eth1 -d 10.1.1.0/24 -p tcp -j ACCEPT
```

Together with the previous examples, the policy is expanding.

```
[root@RHEL5 ~]# iptables -nvL
Chain INPUT (policy DROP 7 packets, 609 bytes)
 pkts bytes target prot opt in    out   source       destination
    0     0 ACCEPT all  --  lo    *     0.0.0.0/0    0.0.0.0/0
    0     0 ACCEPT tcp  --  eth0  *     0.0.0.0/0    0.0.0.0/0   tcp dpt:22
    0     0 ACCEPT tcp  --  eth1  *     10.1.1.0/24  0.0.0.0/0

Chain FORWARD (policy DROP 0 packets, 0 bytes)
 pkts bytes target prot opt in    out   source       destination

Chain OUTPUT (policy DROP 3 packets, 228 bytes)
 pkts bytes target prot opt in    out   source       destination
    0     0 ACCEPT all  --  *     lo    0.0.0.0/0    0.0.0.0/0
    0     0 ACCEPT tcp  --  *     eth0  0.0.0.0/0    0.0.0.0/0   tcp spt:22
    0     0 ACCEPT tcp  --  *     eth1  0.0.0.0/0    10.1.1.0/24
```

11.3.7. iptables save

Use **iptables save** to automatically implement these rules when the firewall is (re)started.

```
[root@RHEL5 ~]# /etc/init.d/iptables save
Saving firewall rules to /etc/sysconfig/iptables:        [  OK  ]
[root@RHEL5 ~]#
```

11.3.8. scripting example

You can write a simple script for these rules. Below is an example script that implements the firewall rules that you saw before in this chapter.

```
#!/bin/bash
# first cleanup everything
iptables -t filter -F
iptables -t filter -X
iptables -t nat -F
iptables -t nat -X

# default drop
iptables -P INPUT DROP
iptables -P FORWARD DROP
iptables -P OUTPUT DROP

# allow loopback device
iptables -A INPUT -i lo -j ACCEPT
iptables -A OUTPUT -o lo -j ACCEPT

# allow ssh over eth0 from outside to system
iptables -A INPUT -i eth0 -p tcp --dport 22 -j ACCEPT
iptables -A OUTPUT -o eth0 -p tcp --sport 22 -j ACCEPT

# allow any traffic from 10.1.1.0/24 to system
iptables -A INPUT -i eth1 -s 10.1.1.0/24 -p tcp -j ACCEPT
iptables -A OUTPUT -o eth1 -d 10.1.1.0/24 -p tcp -j ACCEPT
```

11.3.9. Allowing ICMP(ping)

When you enable iptables, you will get an **'Operation not permitted'** message when trying to ping other hosts.

```
[root@RHEL5 ~# ping 192.168.187.130
PING 192.168.187.130 (192.168.187.130) 56(84) bytes of data.
ping: sendmsg: Operation not permitted
ping: sendmsg: Operation not permitted
```

The screenshot below shows you how to setup iptables to allow a ping from or to your machine.

```
[root@RHEL5 ~]# iptables -A INPUT -p icmp --icmp-type any -j ACCEPT
[root@RHEL5 ~]# iptables -A OUTPUT -p icmp --icmp-type any -j ACCEPT
```

The previous two lines do not allow other computers to route ping messages through your router, because it only handles INPUT and OUTPUT. For routing of ping, you will need to enable it on the FORWARD chain. The following command enables routing of icmp messages between networks.

```
[root@RHEL5 ~]# iptables -A FORWARD -p icmp --icmp-type any -j ACCEPT
```

11.4. practice: packet filtering

1. Make sure you can ssh to your router-system when iptables is active.

2. Make sure you can ping to your router-system when iptables is active.

3. Define one of your networks as 'internal' and the other as 'external'. Configure the router to allow visits to a website (http) to go from the internal network to the external network (but not in the other direction).

4. Make sure the internal network can ssh to the external, but not the other way around.

11.5. solution: packet filtering

A possible solution, where leftnet is the internal and rightnet is the external network.

```
#!/bin/bash

# first cleanup everything
iptables -t filter -F
iptables -t filter -X
iptables -t nat -F
iptables -t nat -X

# default drop
iptables -P INPUT DROP
iptables -P FORWARD DROP
iptables -P OUTPUT DROP

# allow loopback device
iptables -A INPUT -i lo -j ACCEPT
iptables -A OUTPUT -o lo -j ACCEPT

# question 1: allow ssh over eth0
iptables -A INPUT -i eth0 -p tcp --dport 22 -j ACCEPT
iptables -A OUTPUT -o eth0 -p tcp --sport 22 -j ACCEPT

# question 2: Allow icmp(ping) anywhere
iptables -A INPUT -p icmp --icmp-type any -j ACCEPT
iptables -A FORWARD -p icmp --icmp-type any -j ACCEPT
iptables -A OUTPUT -p icmp --icmp-type any -j ACCEPT

# question 3: allow http from internal(leftnet) to external(rightnet)
iptables -A FORWARD -i eth1 -o eth2 -p tcp --dport 80 -j ACCEPT
iptables -A FORWARD -i eth2 -o eth1 -p tcp --sport 80 -j ACCEPT

# question 4: allow ssh from internal(leftnet) to external(rightnet)
iptables -A FORWARD -i eth1 -o eth2 -p tcp --dport 22 -j ACCEPT
iptables -A FORWARD -i eth2 -o eth1 -p tcp --sport 22 -j ACCEPT

# allow http from external(rightnet) to internal(leftnet)
# iptables -A FORWARD -i eth2 -o eth1 -p tcp --dport 80 -j ACCEPT
# iptables -A FORWARD -i eth1 -o eth2 -p tcp --sport 80 -j ACCEPT

# allow rpcinfo over eth0 from outside to system
# iptables -A INPUT -i eth2 -p tcp --dport 111 -j ACCEPT
# iptables -A OUTPUT -o eth2 -p tcp --sport 111 -j ACCEPT
```

11.6. network address translation

11.6.1. about NAT

A NAT device is a router that is also changing the source and/or target ip-address in packets. It is typically used to connect multiple computers in a private address range with the (public) internet. A NAT can hide private addresses from the internet.

NAT was developed to mitigate the use of real ip addresses, to allow private address ranges to reach the internet and back, and to not disclose details about internal networks to the outside.

The nat table in iptables adds two new chains. PREROUTING allows altering of packets before they reach the INPUT chain. POSTROUTING allows altering packets after they exit the OUTPUT chain.

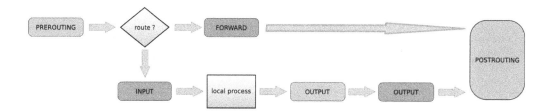

Use **iptables -t nat -nvL** to look at the NAT table. The screenshot below shows an empty NAT table.

```
[root@RHEL5 ~]# iptables -t nat -nL
Chain PREROUTING (policy ACCEPT)
target     prot opt source               destination

Chain POSTROUTING (policy ACCEPT)
target     prot opt source               destination

Chain OUTPUT (policy ACCEPT)
target     prot opt source               destination
[root@RHEL5 ~]#
```

11.6.2. SNAT (Source NAT)

The goal of source nat is to change the source address inside a packet before it leaves the system (e.g. to the internet). The destination will return the packet to the NAT-device. This means our NAT-device will need to keep a table in memory of all the packets it changed, so it can deliver the packet to the original source (e.g. in the private network).

Because SNAT is about packets leaving the system, it uses the POSTROUTING chain.

Here is an example SNAT rule. The rule says that packets coming from 10.1.1.0/24 network and exiting via eth1 will get the source ip-address set to 11.12.13.14. (Note that this is a one line command!)

```
iptables -t nat -A POSTROUTING -o eth1 -s 10.1.1.0/24 -j SNAT \
--to-source 11.12.13.14
```

Of course there must exist a proper iptables filter setup to allow the packet to traverse from one network to the other.

11.6.3. SNAT example setup

This example script uses a typical nat setup. The internal (eth0) network has access via SNAT to external (eth1) webservers (port 80).

```
#!/bin/bash
#
# iptables script for simple classic nat websurfing
# eth0 is internal network, eth1 is internet
#
echo 0 > /proc/sys/net/ipv4/ip_forward
iptables -P INPUT ACCEPT
iptables -P OUTPUT ACCEPT
iptables -P FORWARD DROP
iptables -A FORWARD -i eth0 -o eth1 -s 10.1.1.0/24 -p tcp \
--dport 80 -j ACCEPT
iptables -A FORWARD -i eth1 -o eth0 -d 10.1.1.0/24 -p tcp \
--sport 80 -j ACCEPT
iptables -t nat -A POSTROUTING -o eth1 -s 10.1.1.0/24 -j SNAT \
--to-source 11.12.13.14
echo 1 > /proc/sys/net/ipv4/ip_forward
```

11.6.4. IP masquerading

IP masquerading is very similar to SNAT, but is meant for dynamic interfaces. Typical example are broadband 'router/modems' connected to the internet and receiving a different ip-address from the isp, each time they are cold-booted.

The only change needed to convert the SNAT script to a masquerading is one line.

```
iptables -t nat -A POSTROUTING -o eth1 -s 10.1.1.0/24 -j MASQUERADE
```

11.6.5. DNAT (Destination NAT)

DNAT is typically used to allow packets from the internet to be redirected to an internal server (in your DMZ) and in a private address range that is inaccessible directly form the internet.

This example script allows internet users to reach your internal (192.168.1.99) server via ssh (port 22).

```
#!/bin/bash
#
# iptables script for DNAT
# eth0 is internal network, eth1 is internet
#
echo 0 > /proc/sys/net/ipv4/ip_forward
iptables -P INPUT ACCEPT
iptables -P OUTPUT ACCEPT
iptables -P FORWARD DROP
iptables -A FORWARD -i eth0 -o eth1 -s 10.1.1.0/24 -j ACCEPT
iptables -A FORWARD -i eth1 -o eth0 -p tcp --dport 22 -j ACCEPT
iptables -t nat -A PREROUTING -i eth1 -p tcp --dport 22 \
-j DNAT --to-destination 10.1.1.99
echo 1 > /proc/sys/net/ipv4/ip_forward
```

Part IV. selinux

Table of Contents

Chapter 12. introduction to SELinux

Security Enhanced Linux or **SELinux** is a set of modifications developed by the United States National Security Agency (NSA) to provide a variety of security policies for Linux. SELinux was released as open source at the end of 2000. Since kernel version 2.6 it is an integrated part of Linux.

SELinux offers security! SELinux can control what kind of access users have to files and processes. Even when a file received **chmod 777**, SELinux can still prevent applications from accessing it (Unix file permissions are checked first!). SELinux does this by placing users in **roles** that represent a security context. Administrators have very strict control on access permissions granted to roles.

SELinux is present in the latest versions of Red Hat Enterprise Linux, Debian, CentOS, Fedora, and many other distributions..

12.1. selinux modes

selinux knows three modes: enforcing, permissive and disabled. The **enforcing** mode will enforce policies, and may deny access based on **selinux rules**. The **permissive** mode will not enforce policies, but can still log actions that would have been denied in **enforcing** mode. The **disabled** mode disables **selinux**.

12.2. logging

Verify that **syslog** is running and activated on boot to enable logging of deny messages in **/var/log/messages**.

```
[root@rhel55 ~]# chkconfig --list syslog
syslog          0:off 1:off 2:on 3:on 4:on 5:on 6:off
```

Verify that **auditd** is running and activated on boot to enable logging of easier to read messages in **/var/log/audit/audit.log**.

```
[root@rhel55 ~]# chkconfig --list auditd
auditd          0:off 1:off 2:on 3:on 4:on 5:on 6:off
```

If not activated, then run **chkconfig --levels 2345 auditd on** and **service auditd start**.

```
[root@rhel55 ~]# service auditd status
auditd (pid  1660) is running...
[root@rhel55 ~]# service syslog status
syslogd (pid  1688) is running...
klogd (pid  1691) is running...
```

The **/var/log/messages** log file will tell you that **selinux** is disabled.

```
root@deb503:~# grep -i selinux /var/log/messages
Jun 25 15:59:34 deb503 kernel: [    0.084083] SELinux:  Disabled at boot.
```

Or that it is enabled.

```
root@deb503:~# grep SELinux /var/log/messages | grep -i Init
Jun 25 15:09:52 deb503 kernel: [    0.084094] SELinux:  Initializing.
```

12.3. activating selinux

On RHEL you can use the GUI tool to activate **selinux**, on Debian there is the **selinux-activate** command. Activation requires a reboot.

```
root@deb503:~# selinux-activate
Activating SE Linux
Searching for GRUB installation directory ... found: /boot/grub
Searching for default file ... found: /boot/grub/default
Testing for an existing GRUB menu.lst file ... found: /boot/grub/menu.lst
Searching for splash image ... none found, skipping ...
Found kernel: /boot/vmlinuz-2.6.26-2-686
Updating /boot/grub/menu.lst ... done

SE Linux is activated.  You may need to reboot now.
```

12.4. getenforce

Use **getenforce** to verify whether selinux is **enforced**, **disabled** or **permissive**.

```
[root@rhel55 ~]# getenforce
Permissive
```

The **/selinux/enforce** file contains 1 when enforcing, and 0 when permissive mode is active.

```
root@fedora13 ~# cat /selinux/enforce
1root@fedora13 ~#
```

12.5. setenforce

You can use **setenforce** to switch between the **Permissive** or the **Enforcing** state once **selinux** is activated..

```
[root@rhel55 ~]# setenforce Enforcing
[root@rhel55 ~]# getenforce
Enforcing
[root@rhel55 ~]# setenforce Permissive
[root@rhel55 ~]# getenforce
Permissive
```

Or you could just use 0 and 1 as argument.

```
[root@centos65 ~]# setenforce 1
[root@centos65 ~]# getenforce
Enforcing
[root@centos65 ~]# setenforce 0
[root@centos65 ~]# getenforce
Permissive
[root@centos65 ~]#
```

12.6. sestatus

You can see the current **selinux** status and policy with the **sestatus** command.

```
[root@rhel55 ~]# sestatus
SELinux status:            enabled
SELinuxfs mount:           /selinux
Current mode:              permissive
Mode from config file:     permissive
Policy version:            21
Policy from config file:   targeted
```

12.7. policy

Most Red Hat server will have the **targeted** policy. Only NSA/FBI/CIA/DOD/HLS use the **mls** policy.

The targted policy will protect hundreds of processes, but lets other processes run 'unconfined' (= they can do anything).

12.8. /etc/selinux/config

The main configuration file for **selinux** is **/etc/selinux/config**. When in **permissive** mode, the file looks like this.

The targeted policy is selected in **/etc/selinux/config**.

```
[root@centos65 ~]# cat /etc/selinux/config
# This file controls the state of SELinux on the system.
# SELINUX= can take one of these three values:
#       enforcing - SELinux security policy is enforced.
#       permissive - SELinux prints warnings instead of enforcing.
#       disabled - SELinux is fully disabled.
SELINUX=permissive
# SELINUXTYPE= type of policy in use. Possible values are:
#       targeted - Only targeted network daemons are protected.
#       strict - Full SELinux protection.
SELINUXTYPE=targeted
```

12.9. DAC or MAC

Standard Unix permissions use **Discretionary Access Control** to set permissions on files. This means that a user that owns a file, can make it world readable by typing **chmod 777 $file**.

With **selinux** the kernel will enforce **Mandatory Access Control** which strictly controls what processes or threads can do with files (superseding DAC). Processes are confined by the kernel to the minimum access they require.

SELinux MAC is about labeling and type enforcing! Files, processes, etc are all labeled with an SELinux context. For files, these are extended attributes, for processes this is managed by the kernel.

The format of the labels is as follows:

```
user:role:type:(level)
```

We only use the **type** label in the targeted policy.

12.10. ls -Z

To see the DAC permissions on a file, use **ls -l** to display user and group **owner** and permissions.

For MAC permissions there is new **-Z** option added to **ls**. The output shows that file in **/root** have a XXXtype of **admin_home_t**.

```
[root@centos65 ~]# ls -Z
-rw-------. root root system_u:object_r:admin_home_t:s0 anaconda-ks.cfg
-rw-r--r--. root root system_u:object_r:admin_home_t:s0 install.log
-rw-r--r--. root root system_u:object_r:admin_home_t:s0 install.log.syslog

[root@centos65 ~]# useradd -m -s /bin/bash pol
[root@centos65 ~]# ls -Z /home/pol/.bashrc
-rw-r--r--. pol pol unconfined_u:object_r:user_home_t:s0 /home/pol/.bashrc
```

12.11. -Z

There are also some other tools with the -Z switch:

```
mkdir -Z
cp -Z
ps -Z
netstat -Z
...
```

12.12. /selinux

When selinux is active, there is a new virtual file system named **/selinux**. (You can compare it to /proc and /dev.)

```
[root@centos65 ~]# ls -l /selinux/
total 0
-rw-rw-rw-.  1 root root     0 Apr 12 19:40 access
dr-xr-xr-x.  2 root root     0 Apr 12 19:40 avc
dr-xr-xr-x.  2 root root     0 Apr 12 19:40 booleans
-rw-r--r--.  1 root root     0 Apr 12 19:40 checkreqprot
dr-xr-xr-x. 83 root root     0 Apr 12 19:40 class
--w-------.  1 root root     0 Apr 12 19:40 commit_pending_bools
-rw-rw-rw-.  1 root root     0 Apr 12 19:40 context
-rw-rw-rw-.  1 root root     0 Apr 12 19:40 create
-r--r--r--.  1 root root     0 Apr 12 19:40 deny_unknown
--w-------.  1 root root     0 Apr 12 19:40 disable
-rw-r--r--.  1 root root     0 Apr 12 19:40 enforce
dr-xr-xr-x.  2 root root     0 Apr 12 19:40 initial_contexts
-rw-------.  1 root root     0 Apr 12 19:40 load
-rw-rw-rw-.  1 root root     0 Apr 12 19:40 member
-r--r--r--.  1 root root     0 Apr 12 19:40 mls
crw-rw-rw-.  1 root root 1, 3 Apr 12 19:40 null
-r--------.  1 root root     0 Apr 12 19:40 policy
dr-xr-xr-x.  2 root root     0 Apr 12 19:40 policy_capabilities
-r--r--r--.  1 root root     0 Apr 12 19:40 policyvers
-r--r--r--.  1 root root     0 Apr 12 19:40 reject_unknown
-rw-rw-rw-.  1 root root     0 Apr 12 19:40 relabel
-r--r--r--.  1 root root     0 Apr 12 19:40 status
-rw-rw-rw-.  1 root root     0 Apr 12 19:40 user
```

Although some files in **/selinux** appear wih size 0, they often contain a boolean value. Check **/selinux/enforce** to see if selinux is running in enforced mode.

```
[root@RHEL5 ~]# ls -l /selinux/enforce
-rw-r--r-- 1 root root 0 Apr 29 08:21 /selinux/enforce
[root@RHEL5 ~]# echo $(cat /selinux/enforce)
1
```

12.13. identity

The **SELinux Identity** of a user is distinct from the user ID. An identity is part of a security context, and (via domains) determines what you can do. The screenshot shows user **root** having identity **user_u**.

```
[root@rhel55 ~]# id -Z
user_u:system_r:unconfined_t
```

12.14. role

The **selinux role** defines the domains that can be used. A **role** is denied to enter a domain, unless the **role** is explicitly authorized to do so.

12.15. type (or domain)

The **selinux context** is the security context of a process. An **selinux type** determines what a process can do. The screenshot shows init running in type **init_t** and the mingetty's running in type **getty_t**.

```
[root@centos65 ~]# ps fax -Z | grep /sbin/init
system_u:system_r:init_t:s0        1 ?          Ss      0:00 /sbin/init
[root@centos65 ~]# ps fax -Z | grep getty_t
system_u:system_r:getty_t:s0    1307 tty1       Ss+     0:00 /sbin/mingetty /dev/tty1
system_u:system_r:getty_t:s0    1309 tty2       Ss+     0:00 /sbin/mingetty /dev/tty2
system_u:system_r:getty_t:s0    1311 tty3       Ss+     0:00 /sbin/mingetty /dev/tty3
system_u:system_r:getty_t:s0    1313 tty4       Ss+     0:00 /sbin/mingetty /dev/tty4
system_u:system_r:getty_t:s0    1320 tty5       Ss+     0:00 /sbin/mingetty /dev/tty5
system_u:system_r:getty_t:s0    1322 tty6       Ss+     0:00 /sbin/mingetty /dev/tty6
```

The **selinux type** is similar to an **selinux domain**, but refers to directories and files instead of processes.

Hundreds of binaries also have a type:

```
[root@centos65 sbin]# ls -lZ useradd usermod userdel httpd postcat postfix
-rwxr-xr-x. root root system_u:object_r:httpd_exec_t:s0 httpd
-rwxr-xr-x. root root system_u:object_r:postfix_master_exec_t:s0 postcat
-rwxr-xr-x. root root system_u:object_r:postfix_master_exec_t:s0 postfix
-rwxr-x---. root root system_u:object_r:useradd_exec_t:s0 useradd
-rwxr-x---. root root system_u:object_r:useradd_exec_t:s0 userdel
-rwxr-x---. root root system_u:object_r:useradd_exec_t:s0 usermod
```

Ports also have a context.

```
[root@centos65 sbin]# netstat -nptlZ | tr -s ' ' | cut -d' ' -f6-

Foreign Address State PID/Program name Security Context
LISTEN 1096/rpcbind system_u:system_r:rpcbind_t:s0
LISTEN 1208/sshd system_u:system_r:sshd_t:s0-s0:c0.c1023
LISTEN 1284/master system_u:system_r:postfix_master_t:s0
LISTEN 1114/rpc.statd system_u:system_r:rpcd_t:s0
LISTEN 1096/rpcbind system_u:system_r:rpcbind_t:s0
LISTEN 1666/httpd unconfined_u:system_r:httpd_t:s0
LISTEN 1208/sshd system_u:system_r:sshd_t:s0-s0:c0.c1023
LISTEN 1114/rpc.statd system_u:system_r:rpcd_t:s0
LISTEN 1284/master system_u:system_r:postfix_master_t:s0
```

You can also get a list of ports that are managed by SELinux:

```
[root@centos65 ~]# semanage port -l | tail
xfs_port_t                 tcp      7100
xserver_port_t             tcp      6000-6150
zabbix_agent_port_t        tcp      10050
zabbix_port_t              tcp      10051
zarafa_port_t              tcp      236, 237
zebra_port_t               tcp      2600-2604, 2606
zebra_port_t               udp      2600-2604, 2606
zented_port_t              tcp      1229
zented_port_t              udp      1229
zope_port_t                tcp      8021
```

12.16. security context

The combination of identity, role and domain or type make up the **selinux security context**. The **id** will show you your security context in the form identity:role:domain.

```
[paul@RHEL5 ~]$ id | cut -d' ' -f4
context=user_u:system_r:unconfined_t
```

The **ls -Z** command shows the security context for a file in the form identity:role:type.

```
[paul@RHEL5 ~]$ ls -Z test
-rw-rw-r--  paul paul user_u:object_r:user_home_t       test
```

The security context for processes visible in /proc defines both the type (of the file in /proc) and the domain (of the running process). Let's take a look at the init process and /proc/1/ .

The init process runs in domain **init_t**.

```
[root@RHEL5 ~]# ps -ZC init
LABEL                             PID TTY          TIME CMD
system_u:system_r:init_t            1 ?        00:00:01 init
```

The **/proc/1/** directory, which identifies the **init** process, has type **init_t**.

```
[root@RHEL5 ~]# ls -Zd /proc/1/
dr-xr-xr-x  root root system_u:system_r:init_t          /proc/1/
```

It is not a coincidence that the domain of the **init** process and the type of **/proc/1/** are both **init_t**.

Don't try to use **chcon** on /proc! It will not work.

12.17. transition

An **selinux transition** (aka an selinux labelling) determines the security context that will be assigned. A transition of process domains is used when you execute a process. A transition of file type happens when you create a file.

An example of file type transition.

```
[pol@centos65 ~]$ touch test /tmp/test
[pol@centos65 ~]$ ls -Z test
-rw-rw-r--. pol pol unconfined_u:object_r:user_home_t:s0 test
[pol@centos65 ~]$ ls -Z /tmp/test
-rw-rw-r--. pol pol unconfined_u:object_r:user_tmp_t:s0 /tmp/test
```

12.18. extended attributes

Extended attributes are used by **selinux** to store security contexts. These attributes can be viewed with **ls** when **selinux** is running.

```
[root@RHEL5 home]# ls --context
drwx------  paul paul system_u:object_r:user_home_dir_t paul
drwxr-xr-x  root root user_u:object_r:user_home_dir_t  project42
drwxr-xr-x  root root user_u:object_r:user_home_dir_t  project55
[root@RHEL5 home]# ls -Z
drwx------  paul paul system_u:object_r:user_home_dir_t paul
drwxr-xr-x  root root user_u:object_r:user_home_dir_t  project42
drwxr-xr-x  root root user_u:object_r:user_home_dir_t  project55
[root@RHEL5 home]#
```

When selinux is not running, then **getfattr** is the tool to use.

```
[root@RHEL5 etc]# getfattr -m . -d hosts
# file: hosts
security.selinux="system_u:object_r:etc_t:s0\000"
```

12.19. process security context

A new option is added to **ps** to see the selinux security context of processes.

```
[root@RHEL5 etc]# ps -ZC mingetty
LABEL                           PID TTY          TIME CMD
system_u:system_r:getty_t       2941 tty1     00:00:00 mingetty
system_u:system_r:getty_t       2942 tty2     00:00:00 mingetty
```

12.20. chcon

Use **chcon** to change the selinux security context.

This example shows how to use **chcon** to change the **type** of a file.

```
[root@rhel55 ~]# ls -Z /var/www/html/test42.txt
-rw-r--r--  root root user_u:object_r:httpd_sys_content_t /var/www/html/test4\
2.txt
[root@rhel55 ~]# chcon -t samba_share_t /var/www/html/test42.txt
[root@rhel55 ~]# ls -Z /var/www/html/test42.txt
-rw-r--r--  root root user_u:object_r:samba_share_t    /var/www/html/test42.txt
```

Be sure to read **man chcon**.

12.21. an example

The **Apache2 webserver** is by default targeted with **SELinux**. The next screenshot shows that any file created in **/var/www/html** will by default get the **httpd_sys_content_t** type.

```
[root@centos65 ~]# touch /var/www/html/test42.txt
[root@centos65 ~]# ls -Z /var/www/html/test42.txt
-rw-r--r--. root root unconfined_u:object_r:httpd_sys_content_t:s0 /var/www/h\
tml/test42.txt
```

Files created elsewhere do not get this type.

```
[root@centos65 ~]# touch /root/test42.txt
[root@centos65 ~]# ls -Z /root/test42.txt
-rw-r--r--. root root unconfined_u:object_r:admin_home_t:s0 /root/test42.txt
```

Make sure **Apache2** runs.

```
[root@centos65 ~]# service httpd restart
Stopping httpd:                                           [  OK  ]
Starting httpd:                                           [  OK  ]
```

Will this work ? Yes it does.

```
[root@centos65 ~]# wget http://localhost/test42.txt
--2014-04-12 20:56:47--  http://localhost/test42.txt
Resolving localhost... ::1, 127.0.0.1
Connecting to localhost|::1|:80... connected.
HTTP request sent, awaiting response... 200 OK
Length: 0 [text/plain]
Saving to: "test42.txt"
...
```

Why does this work ? Because Apache2 runs in the **httpd_t** domain and the files in **/var/www/html** have the **httpd_sys_content_t** type.

```
[root@centos65 ~]# ps -ZC httpd | head -4
LABEL                           PID TTY          TIME CMD
unconfined_u:system_r:httpd_t:s0 1666 ?        00:00:00 httpd
unconfined_u:system_r:httpd_t:s0 1668 ?        00:00:00 httpd
unconfined_u:system_r:httpd_t:s0 1669 ?        00:00:00 httpd
```

So let's set SELinux to **enforcing** and change the **type** of this file.

```
[root@centos65 ~]# chcon -t samba_share_t /var/www/html/test42.txt
[root@centos65 ~]# ls -Z /var/www/html/test42.txt
-rw-r--r--. root root unconfined_u:object_r:samba_share_t:s0 /var/www/html/t\
est42.txt
[root@centos65 ~]# setenforce 1
[root@centos65 ~]# getenforce
Enforcing
```

There are two possibilities now: either it works, or it fails. It works when **selinux** is in **permissive mode**, it fails when in **enforcing mode**.

```
[root@centos65 ~]# wget http://localhost/test42.txt
--2014-04-12 21:05:02--  http://localhost/test42.txt
Resolving localhost... ::1, 127.0.0.1
Connecting to localhost|::1|:80... connected.
HTTP request sent, awaiting response... 403 Forbidden
2014-04-12 21:05:02 ERROR 403: Forbidden.
```

The log file gives you a cryptic message...

```
[root@centos65 ~]# tail -3 /var/log/audit/audit.log
type=SYSCALL msg=audit(1398200702.803:64): arch=c000003e syscall=4 succ\
ess=no exit=-13 a0=7f5fbc334d70 a1=7fff553b4f10 a2=7fff553b4f10 a3=0 it\
ems=0 ppid=1666 pid=1673 auid=500 uid=48 gid=48 euid=48 suid=48 fsuid=4\
8 egid=48 sgid=48 fsgid=48 tty=(none) ses=1 comm="httpd" exe="/usr/sbin\
/httpd" subj=unconfined_u:system_r:httpd_t:s0 key=(null)
type=AVC msg=audit(1398200702.804:65): avc:  denied  { getattr } for  p\
id=1673 comm="httpd" path="/var/www/html/test42.txt" dev=dm-0 ino=26324\
1 scontext=unconfined_u:system_r:httpd_t:s0 tcontext=unconfined_u:objec\
t_r:samba_share_t:s0 tclass=file
type=SYSCALL msg=audit(1398200702.804:65): arch=c000003e syscall=6 succ\
ess=no exit=-13 a0=7f5fbc334e40 a1=7fff553b4f10 a2=7fff553b4f10 a3=1 it\
ems=0 ppid=1666 pid=1673 auid=500 uid=48 gid=48 euid=48 suid=48 fsuid=4\
8 egid=48 sgid=48 fsgid=48 tty=(none) ses=1 comm="httpd" exe="/usr/sbin\
/httpd" subj=unconfined_u:system_r:httpd_t:s0 key=(null)
```

And **/var/log/messages** mentions nothing of the failed download.

12.22. setroubleshoot

The log file above was not very helpful, but these two packages can make your life much easier.

```
[root@centos65 ~]# yum -y install setroubleshoot setroubleshoot-server
```

You need to **reboot** for this to work...

So we reboot, restart the httpd server, reactive SELinux Enforce, and do the wget again... and it fails (because of SELinux).

```
[root@centos65 ~]# service httpd restart
Stopping httpd:                                          [FAILED]
Starting httpd:                                          [  OK  ]
[root@centos65 ~]# getenforce
Permissive
[root@centos65 ~]# setenforce  1
[root@centos65 ~]# getenforce
Enforcing
[root@centos65 ~]# wget http://localhost/test42.txt
--2014-04-12 21:44:13--  http://localhost/test42.txt
Resolving localhost... ::1, 127.0.0.1
Connecting to localhost|::1|:80... connected.
HTTP request sent, awaiting response... 403 Forbidden
2014-04-12 21:44:13 ERROR 403: Forbidden.
```

The **/var/log/audit/** is still not out best friend, but take a look at **/var/log/messages**.

```
[root@centos65 ~]# tail -2 /var/log/messages
Apr 12 21:44:16  centos65  setroubleshoot: SELinux is preventing /usr/sbin/h\
ttpd from getattr access on the file /var/www/html/test42.txt. For complete \
SELinux messages. run sealert -l b2a84386-54c1-4344-96fb-dcf969776696
Apr 12 21:44:16  centos65  setroubleshoot: SELinux is preventing /usr/sbin/h\
ttpd from getattr access on the file /var/www/html/test42.txt. For complete \
SELinux messages. run sealert -l b2a84386-54c1-4344-96fb-dcf969776696
```

So we run the command it suggests...

```
[root@centos65 ~]# sealert -l b2a84386-54c1-4344-96fb-dcf969776696
SELinux is preventing /usr/sbin/httpd from getattr access on the file /va\
r/www/html/test42.txt.

*****  Plugin restorecon (92.2 confidence) suggests   *********************

If you want to fix the label.
/var/www/html/test42.txt default label should be httpd_sys_content_t.
Then you can run restorecon.
Do
# /sbin/restorecon -v /var/www/html/test42.txt
...
```

We follow the friendly advice and try again to download our file:

```
[root@centos65 ~]# /sbin/restorecon -v /var/www/html/test42.txt
/sbin/restorecon reset /var/www/html/test42.txt context unconfined_u:objec\
t_r:samba_share_t:s0->unconfined_u:object_r:httpd_sys_content_t:s0
[root@centos65 ~]# wget http://localhost/test42.txt
--2014-04-12 21:54:03--  http://localhost/test42.txt
Resolving localhost... ::1, 127.0.0.1
Connecting to localhost|::1|:80... connected.
HTTP request sent, awaiting response... 200 OK
```

It works!

12.23. booleans

Booleans are on/off switches

```
[root@centos65 ~]# getsebool -a | head
abrt_anon_write --> off
abrt_handle_event --> off
allow_console_login --> on
allow_cvs_read_shadow --> off
allow_daemons_dump_core --> on
allow_daemons_use_tcp_wrapper --> off
allow_daemons_use_tty --> on
allow_domain_fd_use --> on
allow_execheap --> off
allow_execmem --> on
```

You can set and read individual booleans.

```
[root@centos65 ~]# setsebool httpd_read_user_content=1
[root@centos65 ~]# getsebool httpd_read_user_content
httpd_read_user_content --> on
[root@centos65 ~]# setsebool httpd_enable_homedirs=1
[root@centos65 ~]# getsebool httpd_enable_homedirs
httpd_enable_homedirs --> on
```

You can set these booleans permanent.

```
[root@centos65 ~]# setsebool -P httpd_enable_homedirs=1
[root@centos65 ~]# setsebool -P httpd_read_user_content=1
```

The above commands regenerate the complete /etc/selinux/targeted directory!

```
[root@centos65 ~]# cat /etc/selinux/targeted/modules/active/booleans.local
# This file is auto-generated by libsemanage
# Do not edit directly.

httpd_enable_homedirs=1
httpd_read_user_content=1
```

Part V. Appendix

Table of Contents

Appendix A. License

0. PREAMBLE

The purpose of this License is to make a manual, textbook, or other functional and useful document "free" in the sense of freedom: to assure everyone the effective freedom to copy and redistribute it, with or without modifying it, either commercially or noncommercially. Secondarily, this License preserves for the author and publisher a way to get credit for their work, while not being considered responsible for modifications made by others.

This License is a kind of "copyleft", which means that derivative works of the document must themselves be free in the same sense. It complements the GNU General Public License, which is a copyleft license designed for free software.

We have designed this License in order to use it for manuals for free software, because free software needs free documentation: a free program should come with manuals providing the same freedoms that the software does. But this License is not limited to software manuals; it can be used for any textual work, regardless of subject matter or whether it is published as a printed book. We recommend this License principally for works whose purpose is instruction or reference.

1. APPLICABILITY AND DEFINITIONS

This License applies to any manual or other work, in any medium, that contains a notice placed by the copyright holder saying it can be distributed under the terms of this License. Such a notice grants a world-wide, royalty-free license, unlimited in duration, to use that work under the conditions stated herein. The "Document", below, refers to any such manual or work. Any member of the public is a licensee, and is addressed as "you". You accept the license if you copy, modify or distribute the work in a way requiring permission under copyright law.

A "Modified Version" of the Document means any work containing the Document or a portion of it, either copied verbatim, or with modifications and/or translated into another language.

A "Secondary Section" is a named appendix or a front-matter section of the Document that deals exclusively with the relationship of the publishers or authors of the Document to the Document's overall subject (or to related matters) and contains nothing that could fall directly within that overall subject. (Thus, if the Document is in part a textbook of mathematics, a Secondary Section may not explain any mathematics.) The relationship could be a matter of historical connection with the subject or with related matters, or of legal, commercial, philosophical, ethical or political position regarding them.

The "Invariant Sections" are certain Secondary Sections whose titles

are designated, as being those of Invariant Sections, in the notice
that says that the Document is released under this License. If a
section does not fit the above definition of Secondary then it is not
allowed to be designated as Invariant. The Document may contain zero
Invariant Sections. If the Document does not identify any Invariant
Sections then there are none.

The "Cover Texts" are certain short passages of text that are listed,
as Front-Cover Texts or Back-Cover Texts, in the notice that says that
the Document is released under this License. A Front-Cover Text may be
at most 5 words, and a Back-Cover Text may be at most 25 words.

A "Transparent" copy of the Document means a machine-readable copy,
represented in a format whose specification is available to the
general public, that is suitable for revising the document
straightforwardly with generic text editors or (for images composed of
pixels) generic paint programs or (for drawings) some widely available
drawing editor, and that is suitable for input to text formatters or
for automatic translation to a variety of formats suitable for input
to text formatters. A copy made in an otherwise Transparent file
format whose markup, or absence of markup, has been arranged to thwart
or discourage subsequent modification by readers is not Transparent.
An image format is not Transparent if used for any substantial amount
of text. A copy that is not "Transparent" is called "Opaque".

Examples of suitable formats for Transparent copies include plain
ASCII without markup, Texinfo input format, LaTeX input format, SGML
or XML using a publicly available DTD, and standard-conforming simple
HTML, PostScript or PDF designed for human modification. Examples of
transparent image formats include PNG, XCF and JPG. Opaque formats
include proprietary formats that can be read and edited only by
proprietary word processors, SGML or XML for which the DTD and/or
processing tools are not generally available, and the
machine-generated HTML, PostScript or PDF produced by some word
processors for output purposes only.

The "Title Page" means, for a printed book, the title page itself,
plus such following pages as are needed to hold, legibly, the material
this License requires to appear in the title page. For works in
formats which do not have any title page as such, "Title Page" means
the text near the most prominent appearance of the work's title,
preceding the beginning of the body of the text.

The "publisher" means any person or entity that distributes copies of
the Document to the public.

A section "Entitled XYZ" means a named subunit of the Document whose
title either is precisely XYZ or contains XYZ in parentheses following
text that translates XYZ in another language. (Here XYZ stands for a
specific section name mentioned below, such as "Acknowledgements",
"Dedications", "Endorsements", or "History".) To "Preserve the Title"
of such a section when you modify the Document means that it remains a
section "Entitled XYZ" according to this definition.

The Document may include Warranty Disclaimers next to the notice which
states that this License applies to the Document. These Warranty
Disclaimers are considered to be included by reference in this
License, but only as regards disclaiming warranties: any other
implication that these Warranty Disclaimers may have is void and has
no effect on the meaning of this License.

2. VERBATIM COPYING

You may copy and distribute the Document in any medium, either commercially or noncommercially, provided that this License, the copyright notices, and the license notice saying this License applies to the Document are reproduced in all copies, and that you add no other conditions whatsoever to those of this License. You may not use technical measures to obstruct or control the reading or further copying of the copies you make or distribute. However, you may accept compensation in exchange for copies. If you distribute a large enough number of copies you must also follow the conditions in section 3.

You may also lend copies, under the same conditions stated above, and you may publicly display copies.

3. COPYING IN QUANTITY

If you publish printed copies (or copies in media that commonly have printed covers) of the Document, numbering more than 100, and the Document's license notice requires Cover Texts, you must enclose the copies in covers that carry, clearly and legibly, all these Cover Texts: Front-Cover Texts on the front cover, and Back-Cover Texts on the back cover. Both covers must also clearly and legibly identify you as the publisher of these copies. The front cover must present the full title with all words of the title equally prominent and visible. You may add other material on the covers in addition. Copying with changes limited to the covers, as long as they preserve the title of the Document and satisfy these conditions, can be treated as verbatim copying in other respects.

If the required texts for either cover are too voluminous to fit legibly, you should put the first ones listed (as many as fit reasonably) on the actual cover, and continue the rest onto adjacent pages.

If you publish or distribute Opaque copies of the Document numbering more than 100, you must either include a machine-readable Transparent copy along with each Opaque copy, or state in or with each Opaque copy a computer-network location from which the general network-using public has access to download using public-standard network protocols a complete Transparent copy of the Document, free of added material. If you use the latter option, you must take reasonably prudent steps, when you begin distribution of Opaque copies in quantity, to ensure that this Transparent copy will remain thus accessible at the stated location until at least one year after the last time you distribute an Opaque copy (directly or through your agents or retailers) of that edition to the public.

It is requested, but not required, that you contact the authors of the Document well before redistributing any large number of copies, to give them a chance to provide you with an updated version of the Document.

4. MODIFICATIONS

You may copy and distribute a Modified Version of the Document under the conditions of sections 2 and 3 above, provided that you release the Modified Version under precisely this License, with the Modified Version filling the role of the Document, thus licensing distribution and modification of the Modified Version to whoever possesses a copy of it. In addition, you must do these things in the Modified Version:

   * A. Use in the Title Page (and on the covers, if any) a title distinct from that of the Document, and from those of previous versions (which should, if there were any, be listed in the History section of the Document). You may use the same title as a previous version if the original publisher of that version gives permission.

* B. List on the Title Page, as authors, one or more persons or entities responsible for authorship of the modifications in the Modified Version, together with at least five of the principal authors of the Document (all of its principal authors, if it has fewer than five), unless they release you from this requirement.

* C. State on the Title page the name of the publisher of the Modified Version, as the publisher.

* D. Preserve all the copyright notices of the Document.

* E. Add an appropriate copyright notice for your modifications adjacent to the other copyright notices.

* F. Include, immediately after the copyright notices, a license notice giving the public permission to use the Modified Version under the terms of this License, in the form shown in the Addendum below.

* G. Preserve in that license notice the full lists of Invariant Sections and required Cover Texts given in the Document's license notice.

* H. Include an unaltered copy of this License.

* I. Preserve the section Entitled "History", Preserve its Title, and add to it an item stating at least the title, year, new authors, and publisher of the Modified Version as given on the Title Page. If there is no section Entitled "History" in the Document, create one stating the title, year, authors, and publisher of the Document as given on its Title Page, then add an item describing the Modified Version as stated in the previous sentence.

* J. Preserve the network location, if any, given in the Document for public access to a Transparent copy of the Document, and likewise the network locations given in the Document for previous versions it was based on. These may be placed in the "History" section. You may omit a network location for a work that was published at least four years before the Document itself, or if the original publisher of the version it refers to gives permission.

* K. For any section Entitled "Acknowledgements" or "Dedications", Preserve the Title of the section, and preserve in the section all the substance and tone of each of the contributor acknowledgements and/or dedications given therein.

* L. Preserve all the Invariant Sections of the Document, unaltered in their text and in their titles. Section numbers or the equivalent are not considered part of the section titles.

* M. Delete any section Entitled "Endorsements". Such a section may not be included in the Modified Version.

* N. Do not retitle any existing section to be Entitled "Endorsements" or to conflict in title with any Invariant Section.

* O. Preserve any Warranty Disclaimers.

If the Modified Version includes new front-matter sections or appendices that qualify as Secondary Sections and contain no material copied from the Document, you may at your option designate some or all of these sections as invariant. To do this, add their titles to the list of Invariant Sections in the Modified Version's license notice. These titles must be distinct from any other section titles.

You may add a section Entitled "Endorsements", provided it contains nothing but endorsements of your Modified Version by various parties—for example, statements of peer review or that the text has been approved by an organization as the authoritative definition of a standard.

You may add a passage of up to five words as a Front-Cover Text, and a passage of up to 25 words as a Back-Cover Text, to the end of the list of Cover Texts in the Modified Version. Only one passage of Front-Cover Text and one of Back-Cover Text may be added by (or through arrangements made by) any one entity. If the Document already includes a cover text for the same cover, previously added by you or by arrangement made by the same entity you are acting on behalf of, you may not add another; but you may replace the old one, on explicit permission from the previous publisher that added the old one.

The author(s) and publisher(s) of the Document do not by this License give permission to use their names for publicity for or to assert or imply endorsement of any Modified Version.

5. COMBINING DOCUMENTS

You may combine the Document with other documents released under this License, under the terms defined in section 4 above for modified versions, provided that you include in the combination all of the Invariant Sections of all of the original documents, unmodified, and list them all as Invariant Sections of your combined work in its license notice, and that you preserve all their Warranty Disclaimers.

The combined work need only contain one copy of this License, and multiple identical Invariant Sections may be replaced with a single copy. If there are multiple Invariant Sections with the same name but different contents, make the title of each such section unique by adding at the end of it, in parentheses, the name of the original author or publisher of that section if known, or else a unique number. Make the same adjustment to the section titles in the list of Invariant Sections in the license notice of the combined work.

In the combination, you must combine any sections Entitled "History" in the various original documents, forming one section Entitled "History"; likewise combine any sections Entitled "Acknowledgements", and any sections Entitled "Dedications". You must delete all sections Entitled "Endorsements".

6. COLLECTIONS OF DOCUMENTS

You may make a collection consisting of the Document and other documents released under this License, and replace the individual copies of this License in the various documents with a single copy that is included in the collection, provided that you follow the rules of this License for verbatim copying of each of the documents in all other respects.

You may extract a single document from such a collection, and distribute it individually under this License, provided you insert a copy of this License into the extracted document, and follow this License in all other respects regarding verbatim copying of that document.

7. AGGREGATION WITH INDEPENDENT WORKS

A compilation of the Document or its derivatives with other separate and independent documents or works, in or on a volume of a storage or distribution medium, is called an "aggregate" if the copyright resulting from the compilation is not used to limit the legal rights of the compilation's users beyond what the individual works permit. When the Document is included in an aggregate, this License does not apply to the other works in the aggregate which are not themselves derivative works of the Document.

If the Cover Text requirement of section 3 is applicable to these copies of the Document, then if the Document is less than one half of the entire aggregate, the Document's Cover Texts may be placed on covers that bracket the Document within the aggregate, or the electronic equivalent of covers if the Document is in electronic form. Otherwise they must appear on printed covers that bracket the whole aggregate.

8. TRANSLATION

Translation is considered a kind of modification, so you may
distribute translations of the Document under the terms of section 4.
Replacing Invariant Sections with translations requires special
permission from their copyright holders, but you may include
translations of some or all Invariant Sections in addition to the
original versions of these Invariant Sections. You may include a
translation of this License, and all the license notices in the
Document, and any Warranty Disclaimers, provided that you also include
the original English version of this License and the original versions
of those notices and disclaimers. In case of a disagreement between
the translation and the original version of this License or a notice
or disclaimer, the original version will prevail.

If a section in the Document is Entitled "Acknowledgements",
"Dedications", or "History", the requirement (section 4) to Preserve
its Title (section 1) will typically require changing the actual
title.

9. TERMINATION

You may not copy, modify, sublicense, or distribute the Document
except as expressly provided under this License. Any attempt otherwise
to copy, modify, sublicense, or distribute it is void, and will
automatically terminate your rights under this License.

However, if you cease all violation of this License, then your license
from a particular copyright holder is reinstated (a) provisionally,
unless and until the copyright holder explicitly and finally
terminates your license, and (b) permanently, if the copyright holder
fails to notify you of the violation by some reasonable means prior to
60 days after the cessation.

Moreover, your license from a particular copyright holder is
reinstated permanently if the copyright holder notifies you of the
violation by some reasonable means, this is the first time you have
received notice of violation of this License (for any work) from that
copyright holder, and you cure the violation prior to 30 days after
your receipt of the notice.

Termination of your rights under this section does not terminate the
licenses of parties who have received copies or rights from you under
this License. If your rights have been terminated and not permanently
reinstated, receipt of a copy of some or all of the same material does
not give you any rights to use it.

10. FUTURE REVISIONS OF THIS LICENSE

The Free Software Foundation may publish new, revised versions of the
GNU Free Documentation License from time to time. Such new versions
will be similar in spirit to the present version, but may differ in
detail to address new problems or concerns. See
http://www.gnu.org/copyleft/.

Each version of the License is given a distinguishing version number.
If the Document specifies that a particular numbered version of this
License "or any later version" applies to it, you have the option of
following the terms and conditions either of that specified version or
of any later version that has been published (not as a draft) by the
Free Software Foundation. If the Document does not specify a version
number of this License, you may choose any version ever published (not
as a draft) by the Free Software Foundation. If the Document specifies

that a proxy can decide which future versions of this License can be used, that proxy's public statement of acceptance of a version permanently authorizes you to choose that version for the Document.

11. RELICENSING

"Massive Multiauthor Collaboration Site" (or "MMC Site") means any World Wide Web server that publishes copyrightable works and also provides prominent facilities for anybody to edit those works. A public wiki that anybody can edit is an example of such a server. A "Massive Multiauthor Collaboration" (or "MMC") contained in the site means any set of copyrightable works thus published on the MMC site.

"CC-BY-SA" means the Creative Commons Attribution-Share Alike 3.0 license published by Creative Commons Corporation, a not-for-profit corporation with a principal place of business in San Francisco, California, as well as future copyleft versions of that license published by that same organization.

"Incorporate" means to publish or republish a Document, in whole or in part, as part of another Document.

An MMC is "eligible for relicensing" if it is licensed under this License, and if all works that were first published under this License somewhere other than this MMC, and subsequently incorporated in whole or in part into the MMC, (1) had no cover texts or invariant sections, and (2) were thus incorporated prior to November 1, 2008.

The operator of an MMC Site may republish an MMC contained in the site under CC-BY-SA on the same site at any time before August 1, 2009, provided the MMC is eligible for relicensing.

Index

Symbols

A

C

D

E

F

G

H

I

K

L

M

www.ingramcontent.com/pod-product-compliance
Lightning Source LLC
LaVergne TN
LVHW060144070326
832902LV00018B/2940